Urban Design Case Studies

A Service of Urban Design Newsletter

Third Awards Program

Text by Edward K. Carpenter
Introduction by Paul Goldberger

Published by RC Publications, Inc.
Washington, D.C.

LINKED
BARRIER PLANTING ON EXISTING
SLOPE. PRAIRIE ROSE.
BARRIER
JUNIPERS
POPLARS
Emil T. M

110193

Urban Design Case Studies

A Service of Urban Design Newsletter

Third Awards Program

Published by RC Publications, Inc.
6400 Goldsboro Road
Washington, D.C. 20034

Manufactured in USA

First printing 1979

URBAN DESIGN CASE STUDIES
A Service of Urban Design Newsletter
Third Awards Program

Library of Congress Catalogue Card Number 79-84894
ISBN: 0-915734-25-7

RC Publications
President and Publisher: Robert Cadel
Vice President and Editorial Director: Martin Fox
Art Director: Emil Micha
Associate Editor: Lois Heyman

The New Common Wisdom

By Paul Goldberger
Architecture Critic,
The New York Times

I remember hearing it said about four years ago that one of New York City's urban designers, encountering the newly elected Mayor Abraham Beame in an elevator, took advantage of the chance meeting to ask the mayor what role he intended to give the city's Urban Design Group. "The urban design *what*? I never heard of it," the mayor is supposed to have replied.

The story may be apocryphal, but then again, if this *could* have happened four years ago—if a mayor *could* have been ignorant of the urban design efforts, huge as they were, that had been made in his own city—I don't think it could be repeated today. For by now urban design has seeped into our consciousness as never before. There is an irony here, for the 1960s, the period about which Mayor Beame seemed to be so ignorant, were in some ways the heroic period of urban design, the time when the field was organizing itself and setting its goals through such remarkably ambitious undertakings as the New York City urban design effort of the Lindsay administration. But the irony is that, while the 1960s efforts may have been more ambitious, more sweeping in scope, it is in the 1970s that urban design has become part of the common wisdom. The general public, let alone its mayors, no longer expresses quite such puzzlement at the phrase "urban design," and, more important, the notion underlying everything urban designers do—the notion that cities do not consist of isolated objects, but of buildings, streets, and open space working together—is an idea that has come to affect more and more of our planning and design.

What I find most encouraging about these winners is not that they contain a few impressive new ideas (they do, but I will return to that in a moment). It is not the freshest, most unusual things here that I find most remarkable. What *is* extraordinary is how, taken as a whole, all of these winning schemes indicate an immense shift in general attitudes. What was unusual, what was radical, a decade or so ago has now become middle of the road.

Let me take as an example the Skidmore, Owings and Merrill scheme for Sacramento. Here is a large-scale planning project executed by a firm that, with all due respect, I think we can call conservative by today's standards. Now, given most of what Skidmore has traditionally stood for, given most of what large-scale planning in this country has traditionally stood for, this scheme, which integrates state offices with housing and shops, and includes bicycle paths and welcoming, lively open space, represents a considerable advance. Compare it to its logical counterpart, the ter-

rifyingly banal vision of Buck Rogers as state architect, the Albany Mall. One might say, of course, that the difference is in the clients—Jerry Brown's instincts vs. Nelson Rockefeller's—and there is some truth to this. But the difference comes much more from the times. We have learned crucial lessons about the making of cities in the last decade—vital lessons about the need for mixed uses, the need for compatibility with context, the need for visual variety, the need for human scale. It will be a long time before there are any more Brasilias *or* Albany Malls.

We have a new common wisdom today. The notions of Jane Jacobs, of Herbert Gans, of Robert Venturi, to name only a few whose writings in the 1960s were influential in shaping our present attitudes, are not brand new ones. But they have gone from being radical to being mainstream—the center is now where the radicals used to be.

Thus the Skidmore project, and many others among the current winners we might consider in the same category. The Metro North housing in New York by Conklin and Rossant—not dazzlingly new, but consistently intelligent, a sensitive application of civilized notions of what a city should be, with a central pedestrian street that is especially appealing; the Rainbow Center in Niagara Falls by Gruen Associates, where a glass structure is used not to create more of the austere, sterile landscape of most downtowns but a lively, humane and welcoming public garden; Citicorp Center, by Hugh Stubbins and Associates, which shows again how even the most conservative clients have changed. If you doubt this, look at Citicorp's earlier headquarters across the street at 399 Park Avenue, the most mediocre Kahn and Jacobs box.

It is easy to measure a time by its most advanced work; art and architectural history does that well, and there is no other way in which to trace the history of ideas. But it is sometimes more revealing to measure a time by its less advanced work, by its more conservative efforts. Often these bring us closer to the temper of a certain age, and this is where a building like Citicorp is important. To call it conservative, of course, is not really fair—it is far too good to be called that and nothing else. But most of the things that make it significant from an urban design point of view—as opposed to a purely architectural one—are not innovations. Mixed use, public galleria space, and so forth, are all things we have seen before. But we celebrate their presence here because, first, Hugh Stubbins has done them well, and second, because they represent the admission on the part of a conservative client — prodded, to be sure, by a city government—that such things are desirable. This building offers hope because if Citicorp, really at bottom very much a conventional, unimaginative corporate client, finally concedes that this is what it wants a city to be, then progress really *has* been made.

There is another winner that, in a very different way, offers equal cause for optimism: Dundas/Sherbourne housing in Toronto by Barton Myers. Now, this is not overwhelmingly stylish; it does not make us say "wowee" or "whoopee" or whatever. It is handsome, and it is modest in its scale. It is modest in its general intentions—to relate comfortably to the existing 19th-century housing of this Toronto neighborhood, to create high-density without the appearance of it, to bring more housing into the neighborhood without major disruption of the physical fabric. Nothing extraordinary — yet in its immense common sense, it *is* something extraordinary because we have, over the years, seen so little that has represented these sensible, humane values so well.

It is values and attitudes that have shifted, not design per se. I really do think we have come to look at cities as more complex organisms than we once did. It is fashionable these days to put down modern architecture, to speak of its abstract, austere purism unrelated to the real concerns of life. Regardless of the merit of these arguments with respect to architectural design per se—and I think they *do* have merit—they seem unquestionably true with regard to the modern movement's attitude toward urban planning. The Bauhaus—and even more so, Le Corbusier—saw the city as a static object, as a thing to be crafted into physically perfect form and left alone. There was a great deal of rhetoric about social concerns, but it was empty of meaning and nearly devoid of any understanding of human life. The real interest was in the abstract city, the city as pure and perfect physical object.

We do not see it so simply now, and these winners reflect this new view. What I find impressive about them, beyond the fact that they indicate a shift in the mainstream, is the fact that they do not, as a group, represent any particular view of what a city must be. They seem to share the general values of the post-modern time—a respect for physical context, a respect for liveliness, for human scale, for the old as well as the new—but beyond that, there is not all that much that they have in common. The esthetic that informs Charles Moore's and August Perez's Piazza d'Italia in New Orleans is a different one from that of Rogers, Butler, Burgun and Shahine's Lutheran Medical Center in Brooklyn, or

Llewelyn-Davies' Shahestan Pahlavi for Teheran. They all, however, do represent a respect for history in one way or another—in the case of Teheran, in a plan that recalls certain older cities, in the case of Brooklyn, a willingness to see the potential for re-use in an old factory building. In the case of the Piazza d'Italia, we have an exuberant sort of whimsy—loud in its laughter, free of sacred cows, perhaps somewhat shrill but pulsating with a fresh kind of energy. I don't mind the loudness of the Piazza d'Italia; I don't consider it vulgar. But I shudder at the thought that it might become something of a model. For this project, which might be the freshest, in a sense, of all the winners, does not and should not point the way to the future in and of itself.

For one of the crucial aspects of this time is the absence of models, the absence of a sense of certainty and of absolute directions. We no longer believe in the Corbusian dream of the Ville Radieuse, and properly so, and we no longer believe in the Mumfordian dream of the ideal city, and though that one might be more poignant to set aside, it is just as well in that case, too. For if there is any truth to be stated about our time, it is not that modernism is dead, it is that ideology is dead. There is no longer any belief that dogma will do our work for us; there is no longer certainty that there is one true way to the making of cities. We tend to focus now, far more than we did a decade ago, on what *works*—on what makes common sense, whatever the esthetic it represents.

Indeed, I will go so far as to say that the best design minds active today not only reject Le Corbusier as an urban model, they reject Jane Jacobs as well. I occasionally fear—and this is one of the few drawbacks of our time—that Jacobs' attitudes towards cities, attitudes created as a brilliant and effective means of dismantling an outdated ideology, are becoming an ideology, an orthodoxy, of their own. They should not be seen as such, even though they may be right 80 percent of the time. High-rises are *usually* bad, true, but not *always* bad—look at the success of Stuyvesant Town, a success that Jacobs, unfortunately, refuses to acknowledge. Highways are *usually* bad, but not always bad; there are strong urban design arguments to be made in favor of Westway (although I am not sure that they are ultimately convincing). Retail space is usually good, but it needs to be in the right place with the right reason for being—it is not a panacea; I too often fear that today, whenever a street or plaza or a single building seems wanting, we cry "retail" and think everything is solved by putting in a lot of shops, as sure as Mies thought he was solving everything by taking them out.

It is never so simple. But by saying that we should focus on what works, I don't want to imply that I think we are in, or should be in, a functionalist period. Functionalism is not what I am talking about when I say that we are looking for what works—because for us today, the definition of what works, the criteria for success, are far broader than they were before. For something to "work" now it must fulfill a far broader program than it had to do a decade or two ago—we are far more concerned about buildings working as part of greater physical wholes, as part of social organisms, as part of sensory perception. We are finally beginning to realize that the modern movement served neither the needs of our cities—it wanted to destroy them—nor the needs of our senses—it wanted to ignore them. Today, I think, we value, even celebrate, the sensory aspect of buildings and cities, and we have come to consider these aspects crucial to successful urban design—witness two such dramatically different projects as Rainbow Center Mall and Winter Garden and Piazza d'Italia. Different esthetics, different forms, different programs—but both extremely conscious of our sensory needs in a way that the so-called "plazas" of an earlier urban renewal generation, places like Constitution Plaza in Hartford and Prudential Center in Boston, were not.

So there are many routes to civilized cities, to pleasurable ones, in this non-ideological age. The absence of any automatic dogma, of any neat formulas, can cause problems—in the worst scenario it can lead to chaos. But in a more ideal sequence of events it can free us to get in touch with the basics of urban design and the making of cities — to make decisions on the basis of what makes common sense, not on the basis of what fits into some sort of abstract formula.

There used to be a lot of talk, back when modernism was "hot," of the "spirit of the times." Buildings that were old, or looked like buildings that were old, were considered invalid—they did not match the spirit of the time. Now, we know how shallow such notions are—they pretend to profundity but mean, in the final analysis, very little. The spirit of the time right now is that there is not a single spirit of the time—there are many streams, all flowing in different directions. There are no guidelines, no rules, no certainties. It is a hard time to be an architect or an urban designer, for the models aren't there as they were in the days when modernism's ideology was unshakeable, and you knew you could always win with a glass box and a plaza out front. But such time as the present allows us one real advantage—there is no way of measuring things against an abstract set of rules now, and so things—quality—can be judged on their own merits. We are freer to evaluate streets, buildings, entire cities, on the basis of what works, and on the basis of what gives us pleasure. So if the spirit of the time is anything, it is a respect for quality and a respect for common sense. These were basic to the making of the best parts of the old cities we know and love—and they seem, at long last, to be becoming basic again today, too.

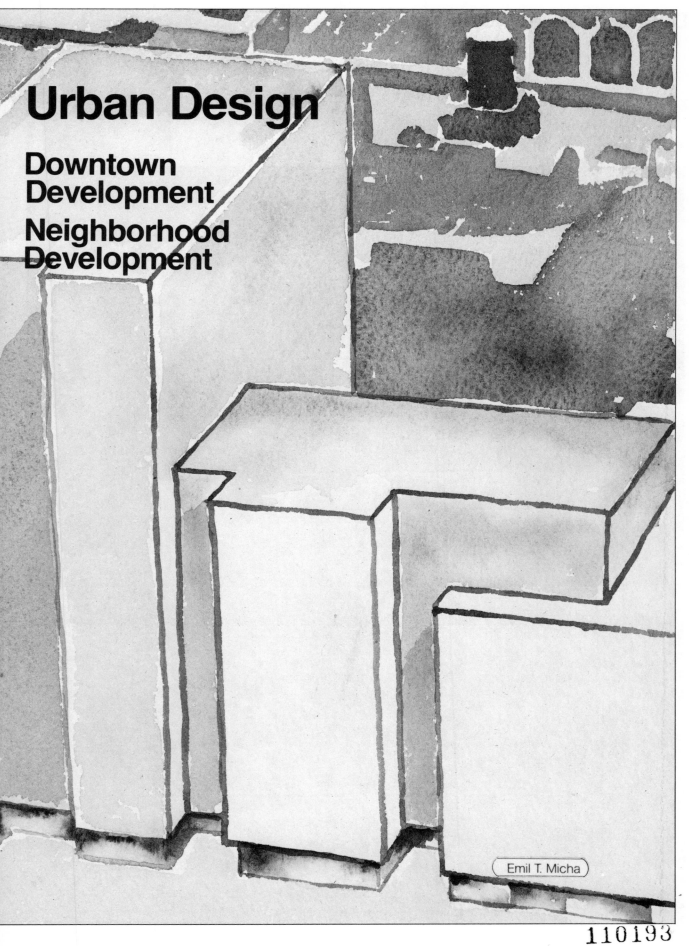

Urban Design

Downtown Development

Neighborhood Development

Emil T. Micha

Downtown Development

**Rainbow Center Mall
and Winter Garden**
Niagara Falls, N.Y.

Designers: Gruen Assoc., architects: Beda Zwicker, partner-in-charge; Abbott Harle, partner-in-charge of technical development; Cesar Pelli, partner-in-charge of design, Gary Engel, director of design, project designer; Thomas W. Loosbrock, project architect. M. Paul Friedberg and Partners, landscape architects

Client: Niagara Falls Urban Renewal Agency

Niagara Falls (both the waterfall and the town next to it) is bleak in the winter, cold, windswept, snowy. The tourists go home. Residents shop at the shopping center outside town. What the city of Niagara Falls needed was something to lure tourists (and residents) year-round, something that would serve as a focal point for downtown, and encourage private development near the city convention center and Overlook Park.

So, with urban renewal funds, the city created a mall and on the mall a year-round garden of subtropical plants. Housed in a steel and glass pavilion reminiscent of Britain's Crystal Palace, the Winter Garden (1) sits midway between the convention center and the park. Joining the latter two and running through the Winter Garden (3) is the landscaped mall (see plan).

The idea is that private developers would build on either side of the mall, using the Winter Garden as an all-weather, two-level connection to their buildings. And the idea seems to have worked. Already underway adjacent to the mall is a Native American Cultural Center. A 240,000 sq. ft. shopping center and a 200,000 sq. ft. corporate office building are in the works. The city plans to sweeten this lure by putting up a 1,700-car parking facility and tying it to the shopping center.

The Winter Garden's glass curtain walls cascade from a peak of 100 ft. to cover a ground area of 175 ft. by 155 ft. Steel framework bridges, elevators and stairs provide circulation (2) on two levels and will eventually attach to two levels of the adjacent development. In the meantime, the Winter Garden's north and south street-level and mezzanine facades are covered by metal panels in winter and left open in summer. Seven thousand five hundred plants and trees, some rising 60 ft., fill the interior space. There is a waterfall. An amphitheater which can seat 100 persons for performances rises above a stage in a pool (4), and in the building's northwest corner is an arid garden with cacti and other desert plants set in a gravel mulch. Along the mall, reaching out east and west from the winter garden, the landscape architects planted rows of maples and pears to give a display of blossoms in the spring and colored foliage in the fall.

The Gallery At Market East
Philadelphia, Pa.

Designers: Bower and Fradley, architects (succeeded by Bower Fradley Lewis Thrower): John A. Bower, Jr., partner-in-charge of design, Roger B. Lewis and Robert T. Mannel, project architects. Collins DuTot Partnership, landscape architects. RTKL, graphic and Market Fair design. Wilbur Smith and Assoc., vehicular design

Client: Redevelopment Authority of the City of Philadelphia, owner. The Rouse Co., Columbia, Md., developer.

The secret, of course, is to have lots going on. And for the Gallery at Market East in downtown Philadelphia it is not just its bazaar-like atmosphere that attracts people. People attract people. And some of them are there by design. Some *must* move through the space. A subway stop empties into the Gallery and there is talk of plugging the Gallery into a new terminal for rail commuters. Flows of people add not only to the allure but also to the feeling of security, and the Gallery's architecture by Bower Fradley Lewis Thrower of Philadelphia means to make it easy for Gallery visitors to see people, people flowing up and down the retail space's 16 escalators, linking 122 shops and restaurants on four levels around a central landscaped, skylighted mall; people sitting beneath trees next to fountains **(4)**; people standing at railings overlooking shoppers moving through the space **(2,3)**. This space, though arranged much as it would be were the Gallery a suburban shopping center, is more compact. The entire project, including two department store anchors, Gimbel's **(1)** and Strawbridge and Clothier, covers only 2.2 acres, small by suburban standards. But space is gained by building up, creating four inside levels instead of the usual suburban two, and by digging down for truck access and unloading. Not counting the department stores, the Gallery has some 200,000 sq. ft. of retail space in a gross area of 400,000 sq. ft. Unlike a conventional shopping center, more of the leased space is occupied by restaurants, 30 percent versus 20 percent in the suburbs, reacting to the hunger of nearby office workers who don't go home for lunch.

There is talk of putting up a hotel in air rights above the Gallery, making the complex more like Chicago's Water Tower Place and Kansas City's Crown Center, which have hotels and offices as well as shopping. But the point of the Gallery is that it uses a concept that has worked so well in the suburbs that it has shaped the way many Americans shop. Many people think of malls when they think of shopping, and this attitude is borne out by figures gathered by the Rouse Company, which paid a third of the construction costs (the Redevelopment Authority put up the other two-thirds) in return for a 99-year leasehold interest. These figures suggest that the average age of a Gallery shopper is 34 years. Before the Gallery opened, the average age of shoppers at the two department stores was 42. The Gallery is luring people who weren't shopping in the area before. And it is luring them in droves. During a typical Christmas season retailers chalk up sales of about $250 a square foot, twice what can be expected in a suburban mall. These sales figures more than offset the increased costs of doing business in the city, and if the success continues, the urban shopping mall will no doubt become a city fixture.

Toronto Eaton Centre
Ontario, Canada

Designers: Bregman and Hamann, architects: Sidney Bregman, executive partner. Zeidler Partnership, architects: Eberhard H. Zeidler, design partner

Clients: The Cadillac Fairview Corporation, The T. Eaton Co. Ltd., The Toronto-Dominion Bank

Covering an area the size of New York's Times Square in downtown Toronto, the Toronto Eaton Centre, a suburban-type shopping center (1), is raising spirits and cash. Already the $250-million project has influenced the life of the city. It is attracting tourists and a good number of the area's 200,000 office workers. Each day some 100,000 persons enter the center and an amazing 74 percent of these buy something, if only a newspaper. By careful arrangement with the city, two subway lines have stops with entrances into the mall. Moreover, a 26-story office building is part of the complex, and a second office tower (27 stories) is planned for the opposite end of the mall. Eaton's department store, already part of the project, may eventually be tied by bridge and underground passage to Simpson's department store to the north.

On the site since 1847, Trinity Church is still there, though the developers, Cadillac Fairview Corporation Ltd., had originally wanted to remove it. It is an obvious part of the area's attraction. A series of pedestrian mews will connect it to a future part of the development.

All this activity, as you might expect, is having an effect on downtown Toronto's appearance. Buildings nearby are sprucing up, and the corner of Dundas and Yonge, where a glassed-in galleria (4) with restaurants, subway entrances, shopping, office space and vendors leads into the Centre, is an inviting lure for the Centre and a focal point for the area.

Elsewhere, the Centre does not relate so well to the surrounding streets (2), and this physical relationship with the city is one of the problems future urban shopping centers must confront. Some arrangement allowing passersby to enter shops from both the street and the interior mall would help both shops and the neighborhood. More glass along side streets so passersby could see the action inside would spur better rapport between neighborhood and center.

The Toronto Eaton Centre is capped by a long arching glass roof (3), making it reminiscent of ancient gallerias such as Damascus's street called Straight.

Ten years of research and public debate went into the center; the city, which worked with the developers and their consultants to set rigorous standards for such measures as density and scale, feels it has established a prototype for other large urban projects.

1

Piazza d'Italia
New Orleans, La.

Designers: August Perez and Assoc., architects: R. Allen Eskew, Malcolm Heard, Jr., project designers; Robert Kleinpeter, project coordinator; Robert Landry, field representative. Fountain design: Charles W. Moore, Urban Innovations Group: Ron Filson, project coordinator. Charles Caplinger Planners, landscape architects.

Client: Office of the Mayor, New Orleans, La.

New Orlean's Piazza d'Italia will, when complete, lie between Poydras Street and the proposed Lafayette Mall only a few blocks from the riverfront and from the Vieux Carre. Meant as a memorial to the achievements of Italian-Americans, it is an inviting circular space, cut like a hole in a square donut from the block of buildings that will surround it **(1)**. These buildings immediately surrounding the piazza are a blend of old and new, five of them 19th-century warehouse structures, the rest only now being put up with floor heights, window placements and proportions matching those of the older structures. No fewer than five passageways lead from the surrounding streets into the piazza (see site plan). Each of these landscaped passages either narrows before opening dramatically onto the piazza or is restrained from above (the entrance off Lafayette Mall passes through an arched passageway in the surrounding buildings). So one's actual arrival in the open piazza is abrupt and effective.

The space becomes suitably and proudly Italian, in a city whose architecture is French, Spanish and, increasingly, 20th-century American. Paving is concentric circles of slate, (dark) and granite (light) moving into the piazza's focus, a marvelous, lighthearted fountain formed of walls depicting the classical architectural orders **(3)**. Water highlights many of the architectural elements, forming egg and dart patterns on one of the entablatures, cascading down the column's flutes to pour over marble bases and into holding pools (lakes), from which the water flows down mirrored rivers over a granite and slate relief map of Italy. The surrounding seas become pools, and the whole map is meant to be a stage (with the water drained). Sicily becomes a rostrum and Sardinia provides seating.

Throughout the architectural elements are mirrors and neon lights, and the effect is festive. It is meant to be. The New Orleans Italian-American community sees the piazza as the focal point of many celebrations, such as Mardi Gras and St. Joseph's Day, March 19th, when massive altars of food are prepared for distribution to the poor.

Rentable portions of the project are being put up by the city, which expects to have restaurants, a delicatessen, and shops selling Italian goods, facing both the surrounding streets **(2)** and the piazza.

A 60 ft.-high campanile rises at one corner of the site as a sort of gesture **(4)** to the 22-story Lykes office and its peers along Poydras Street.

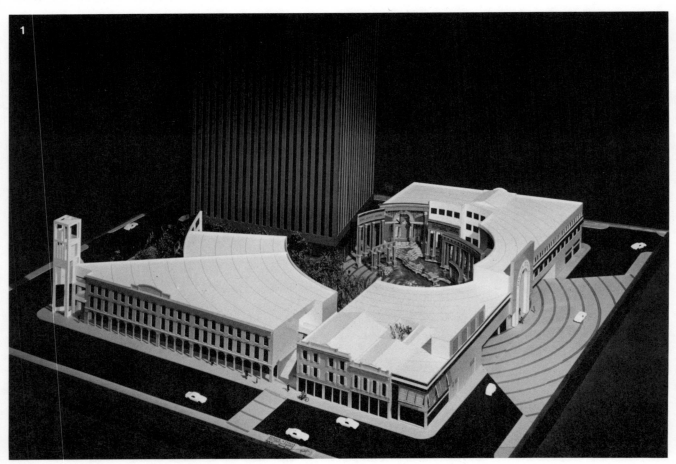

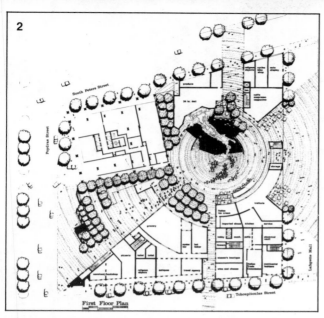

Westlake Park
Seattle, Wash.

Designers: Mitchell/Giurgola, architects. Joyce, Copeland, Vaughan and Nordfors, associate architects

Clients: Mondev International and City of Seattle

Westlake Park, Seattle's first downtown shopping mall, will be set in the midst of three existing department stores and connected to each of them by enclosed bridges. According to the architects, Mitchell/Giurgola, the "primary objective of the design was to create public spaces which will improve the quality of urban life while contributing to the vitality of the downtown retail core." The City of Seattle, of course, shares this objective and has agreed to purchase the land (several small triangular parcels and an unused diagonal street) and finance the pedestrian mall and public spaces. On a triangular lot across from the shopping complex will be a public garden **(1)**, a landscaped open space leading to the glassed southern end of the retail mall the way a formal Italian garden might lead to a villa. Behind the historic Times Square building on the site's northern edge will be a plaza, planned as a sculpture garden, visible through the glassed-in northern end of the retail space **(2)**. From these exterior plazas, at either end of the complex, approaching pedestrians will be able to see shoppers moving up escalators and through the mall. And a new terminal for Seattle's monorail will be partially visible through glass windows along the building's eastern facade **(3)**.

Westlake Park will relate to its surroundings perhaps better than any other downtown mall in the U. S. today. In scale and texture, it is planned to match almost exactly the surrounding structures. It is a concrete building with glazed tile covering at street level. Along 4th and 5th Avenues, pedestrians will look into its shops through large expanses of glass. Retailers renting this ground-level space will have a clause in their leases preventing them from presenting a blank wall to the street. Some of these shops will extend through from street to interior mall. But because the site slopes steeply, shops along 5th Avenue are a full story below the mall. Here, shopkeepers will have an option of leasing space facing street or mall only or space with a loft, facing both ways.

A recent proposal by Seattle's mayor, approved by the city council, substitutes a new home for the Seattle Art Museum for the hotel originally planned above the three retail levels. According to the architects, there is enough space in the structure, as they designed it, to accommodate the museum. The size of the upper space will not change, only its shape and use.

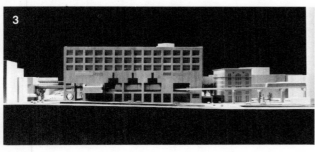

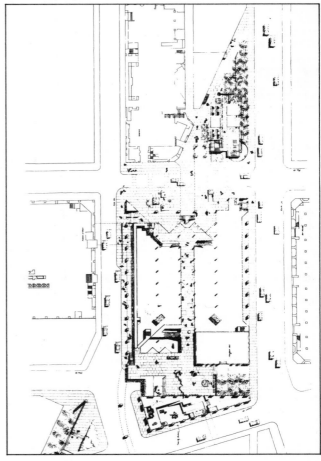

Shahestan Pahlavi
A New City Center for
Tehran, Iran

Designers: Llewelyn-Davies
Assoc.: Jaquelin T.
Robertson, project director;
Christopher J. Glaister,
deputy project director;
Francis Tibbalds, principal
architect-planner; Terrance R.

Williams, principal architect;
Robert W. Ponte, principal
planner; Frank S. Fish, senior
land-use planner; Stephen
Anderson, Farhang Asgari,
John Bowers, Frank Gilmore,
Franklin Israel, Stephen Katz,
Douglas and Dorothea King,
Leon Ross, principal design
team

Client: Sherkat Sahami
Nosazi

Follow-through has been traditionally important in golf and tennis, but it is just as important in urban design. Follow-through is what a significantly ambitious plan for providing Tehran, Iran, with a new city center will need. However, at the time of this book's going-to-press, there was no indication of whether this plan will be able to be implemented, in light of the country's recent political turmoil; whether as Shahestan or the area's original name, Abbasabad, the plan can provide a bold, elegant urban core, with grand public spaces, protected pedestrian spaces and good traffic circulation. Exactly in the city's center are, almost providentially, 1,200 acres of vacant land which can be used for this new urban center without destruction of existing buildings and without the high cost in money and human misery of displacing people. There is nothing on this land; it is an area of barren hills, owned until recently by the military, slated for housing for retired army personnel.

Victor Gruen and Asiz Farman-Farmaian's 1968 master plan for Tehran pinpointed the site as a logical one for a new urban center, and a recently completed plan by Llewelyn-Davies International details how the site can be transformed. This most recent plan is eclectic and bold, drawing on many traditional urban design practices and incorporating a wealth of Persian tradition. It calls, for instance, for a large public square of 80,000 sq. ft. **(1)**, as large as Maidan-e-Shah in Isfahan, six and a half times as large as Venice's Piazza San Marco, and five times larger than Rome's Piazza Del Popolo. A square is obviously traditional, popular in both East and West, but this one will have a special Persian touch. It will be surrounded by a three-story arcade, through and on top of which people can walk the square's perimeter. Within the arcade, the planners foresee a welter of shops, tea houses, restaurants and sitting spaces. "It acts as an extended sidewalk and sitting room around the big square," states Jaquelin T. Robertson, project director for Llewelyn-Davies's Shahestan Pahlavi plan. On top of the arcade is an open walkway and off this walk, on the arcade roof, are a series of sitting spaces, partitioned but roofless, with windows overlooking the square. In these rooms are miniature gardens with flowers and fountains, sunken benches and perhaps even chess tables. These rooms, small spaces on the edge of a large one, are purely Iranian in tradition, and, says Robertson, "one of the nicest qualities of Iranian cities." Behind the arcade, which will serve as a sort of a garden wall while the buildings around the square are being built, will be cultural and government structures. Already, international competitions have been announced for a library and a new city hall, and a new Museum of Modern Art has recently opened.

A major traffic artery leads through and from the square,

linking parks at either end of Shahestan Pahlavi. Flanking the east side of this major spine is a tree-shaded walk, a broad park-like strip with stepped terraces leading up to the square **(2)**. The planners envision the traffic artery as a ceremonial and commercial boulevard not unlike the Champs Elysees or the Chahar Bagh in Isfahan. Housing goes along the parks, lining this spine and other broad arteries paralleling it. Housing will also overlook parks at the edge of Shahestan Pahlavi, where the new center meets the rest of the city. Open space will make up about 40 percent of the new center and an estimated 35-40,000 persons will live there. The way the planners use the land follows its form: major roads are in natural valleys, which need minimum cutting and filling. Buildings for the most part will be confined to the sloping central plain, on land higher than the roads and directly over the right of way of the newly planned metro. Ridges will be left as they are except for walkways with city views.

Shahestan Pahlavi is also meant as a commercial center, replacing the old bazaar, which worked well 50 years ago, and the shopping areas which have grown at inconvenient distances from the center of town. It is appropriate that the shopping center envisioned by the planners is much the same as a large suburban U. S. shopping mall, for these malls in their arrangement are almost identical to traditional Iranian bazaars. Individual developers will be expected to fill in pieces of the shopping mall, building it slowly of large and small shops. This mall would run along the boulevards, behind the housing and offices fronting the boulevards' linear parks, ending at a commercial plaza south of the great square.

Tehran's present commercial and business center is simply too choked with cars and buildings to serve as the city center of the future, and as the planners point out, many cities flourish with two commercial and institutional areas. New York, for example, has downtown and midtown commercial concentrations and London has the old city and Westminster, each contributing to the life of the city. But these comparisons with the West will be modified, for the planners set controls that do away with towering glass-clad skyscrapers. Instead, Shahestan Pahlavi will have lower-scale buildings built around cool courtyards. As with any plan, good architecture will enhance it. But the plan and its controls will, thinks Jaquelin Robertson, make the city work well regardless of the quality of the architecture. "We think that you can make a good city if the open spaces, planting, roads, and pedestrian systems are well designed. Great architecture will make it distinguished."

**Urban Design Element,
Capitol Area Plan**
Sacramento, Calif.

Designers: Skidmore,
Owings and Merrill: John
Kriken, project director;
Thomas Aidala, Barbara
Maloney, Joel Tomei,
principal staff.

Client: Office of State
Architect, California

By the turn of the century, Sacramento, California's capital city, will need an estimated additional two million sq. ft. of government office space. Though this estimate is lower than it was in 1960, when first made, it is obviously substantial, and the city is moving towards doing something about it. An earlier attempt, in the 1960s, saw 75 acres of state-owned land cleared of the homes and shops that stood on it. Perhaps fortunately, renewal moved slowly in the '60s, and only three office buildings went up; the remaining land was finally paved for parking. The delay gave Sacramento officials time to think about renewal, about how they wanted the city reformed—to decide that the city should be much what it once was, with a homogenization of housing, offices, shops, recreation, restaurants, parks. The formation of this planning policy and ways of designing for it are put forth in a document called the Urban Design Element of the Capitol Area Plan, a sort of pre-plan planning guide.

Though much of the Element is suggestive, a good deal of it is concrete. Its aims are direct:

1. to accommodate the state's office building needs without overwhelming the scale and character of historic Sacramento;

2. to make downtown Sacramento once again a good place to work and live, and

3. to make the city symbolic, as a state capital should be, and at the same time attractive and accessible to everyone.

The framework through which the Element proposes to accomplish these often-stated but too-seldom-achieved goals is specific. Basic are two mandates, one regarding size, the other height: an area being developed as a single unit can be no larger than a quarter block (160 ft. by 160 ft.) and no structure can rise higher than four stories **(1)**.

These criteria insure that new development will be in scale with existing downtown Sacramento; and by having four development parcels on each block the way is cleared for mixed uses of the land. Housing can stand next to commercial space and shops **(2)**, and in this way the planners hope to keep the capitol area humming with activity day and night. More than that, by working on just a quarter block at a time, the state can add its office space bit by bit, without further disrupting downtown Sacramento.

As envisioned by planners Skidmore, Owings and Merrill, future building will pay a great deal of attention to open green space, courtyards, small parks, common gardens, tucked in among the new buildings and along streets **(3)**, and their plan works towards less dependence on today's energy sources and on the automobile.

Trails for bikes and pedestrians will wind through the city **(4)** and buildings will be sited to take advantage of sun and shade. Indeed, one of the first new state office structures approved under the Urban Design Element will be partially below grade—its offices lighted by reflective light courts and heated and cooled by the sun.

Overseeing development of the Urban Design Element and the resulting Capitol Area Plan was a Capitol Area Plan Advisory Committee. This committee, made up of state officials, city and county agency representatives and neighborhood spokesmen, looked over the planners' shoulders as planning went on, letting them know what the city wanted.

1

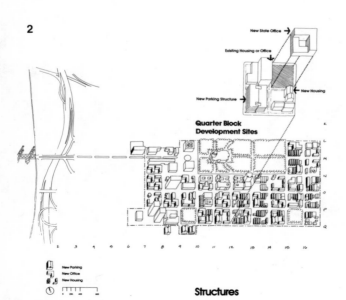

1. Capitol
2. Capitol Park
3. Existing Office
4. Existing Commercial
5. Existing Housing
6. New Office
7. New Housing
8. Hotel

'O' Street
landscaped mall

11th Street
landscaped mall

13th Street
landscaped mall

2

New State Office

Existing Housing or Office

New Parking Structure

New Housing

**Quarter Block
Development Sites**

New Parking
New Office
New Housing

Structures

3

Porch for office
circulation and sun
control

Operating windows

arcade

Courtyard fountain
and landscape

Cafe entered from
street and opening
on courtyard

4

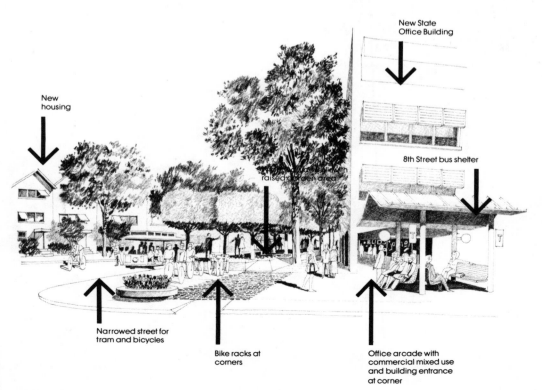

New State
Office Building

New
housing

raised garden area

8th Street bus shelter

Narrowed street for
tram and bicycles

Bike racks at
corners

Office arcade with
commercial mixed use
and building entrance
at corner

City Options: Street Revitalization, New York, N.Y.

Designers: New York City Planning Commission: Edward L. Cohen, project coordinator, "City Options" and project director, Alexander Avenue, Chinatown, Union Square; Carlos Tejada, assistant project urban designer, Alexander Ave.; Shirley S. Passow, co-project director, Chinatown and chief planner, Union Square; Pongporn Sudbanthad, Soothorn Boonyatikarn, assistant project urban designers, Union Square and Chinatown; Joan C. Wallick, project director, Montague Street; Marilyn Gelber, project planner; Robin Burns, project urban designer. Phil Sacks, Henry Nicholas, graphic coordination.

1

One of four small-scale projects chosen by the New York City Planning Department because it could be undertaken without city capital and yet make a significant improvement in part of the city, the Union Square Street Revitalization has moved the farthest toward realization and has the best chance for completion.

Once a thriving, fashionable city hub, with theaters and restaurants, Union Square is today drab and seedy. Even the soapbox debaters who for decades argued the day's issues in the park (slavery in the 1850s and women's rights in the early 1900s) have moved elsewhere, and the park stands surrounded by blurred, rumbling lines of traffic that make it difficult, if not dangerous, to reach. But many of the neighborhood's businesses have stayed. Con Edison's headquarters are a block away; S. Klein's, the discount house that operated on 14th Street and the Square for 63 years, is being leased and refurbished by a new tenant. May's department store is there, along with headquarters for several local unions. Yeshiva University is within a few blocks, and so are Washington Irving and Stuyvesant Highs. Beth Israel Hospital is two blocks to the east.

The 3.59 acres of Union Square Park could become a focal point for the community, argued the city planning commission, if it could be made easily accessible and attractive. In the 1930s the park bed was raised five feet to make room for a mezzanine above the 14th Street subway station. This elevation and the resulting surrounding wall would isolate the park even without the constant swirl of traffic surrounding Union Square like a moat. The city planning department's report suggests changing traffic patterns around the square. It is not the number of vehicles, they claim, that creates the problem, it is their seeming lack of direction, and this can be smoothed out by routing traffic one way, counterclockwise, about the square (1). In conjunction, they would remove parking spaces at the edge of the square, and encourage a private developer to build a garage at the park's north end, where there is now metered parking for 85 cars. A garage roof, the report points out, might be used for recreation such as tennis or basketball. Part of the space gained by removing street parking could be used to widen the park, grading it down to the present curb and removing the wall (2). A traffic island at the southeast corner could be sodded and dotted with food kiosks. Furthermore, a renovated amphitheater podium at the park's northern edge could become a café or a music center, a place continuously used (3).

Community backing is, of course, the key to realizing this plan. Already a consortium of area business and civic organizations, the Union Square Improvement Committee, has raised $1.2 million by pledging $150,000 themselves and using it as leverage with state and federal governments. During the first year they are concentrating on the subway station beneath the square. Says Charles F. Luce, chairman of the board of Con Edison and co-chairman of the 14th Street-Union Square Area Project, "This is not just a use of graphics but a complete remodeling so that subway users will have improved lighting and safe, efficient travel."

3

UNION SQUARE AMPHITHEATRE ●

2

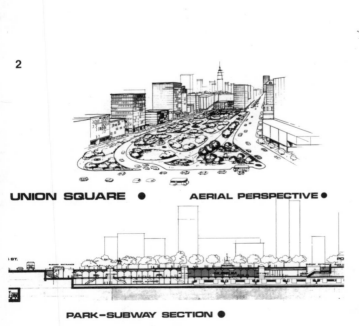

UNION SQUARE ●   **AERIAL PERSPECTIVE** ●

PARK–SUBWAY SECTION ●

UNION SQUARE EAST SECTION-ELEVATION   1 : 20

Pickering Town Centre
Ontario, Canada

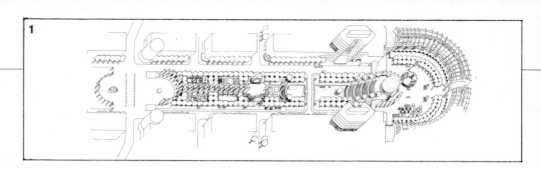

At a time when the enclosed downtown shopping mall is the fad, with more and more cities turning to them as a panacea for urban ills, a team of Canadian planners and architects is boldly proposing a downtown plan with a formal center: an open, tree-lined mall with shopping, houses, offices and recreation space grouped around it.

At the moment, Pickering, Ontario, has no real downtown. Though 25,000 persons live there, the town is composed of three areas of housing and one of industry, poorly connected with one another. What shopping there is lies mostly along highway 401. If they want, Pickering residents can go a few miles west into Toronto for french fries or clothes.

The plan states nine objectives—among them creating an active, year-round, 24-hour-a-day town center, linking it to the existing communities and the communities with one another. Other objectives are to give Pickering, through its town center, a strong image and to create a pattern for future growth. A park network is to be an element of this new center, and so is housing.

Initial emphasis should be on developing shops, along what will become a central mall (1). And, the plan stresses, a first phase of the mall must be buildings around the plaza which bulges from the west end of the mall. These buildings could contain shops with apartments above them, or simply shops, perhaps anchored by department stores on either side of the plaza.

Designers: Zeidler Partnership, urban design consultants: Eberhard H. Zeidler, partner-in-charge; Paul Cravit, Ken Long, Jo Rohn, design team. Ian Macpherson Assoc. Ltd.,

architects: Ian D. Macpherson, project director; Peter R. Walker, project coordinator and land-use planner. Brad Johnson, Johnson Sustronk, Weinstein and Assoc., landscape architects

Client: Town of Pickering

The plan is very specific about where everything should go as the town grows. Designated are areas for commerce, parks, industry, housing, roads and bike paths.

And a final section specifies controls to ensure that the design objectives are met. For example, the purpose of an esplanade park, running down the center of the town mall, is both to create a year-round park for everyone and to form a link between the structures and activities on either side of it. Controls for its construction are very specific indeed, down to type and size of tree. "The double row of trees on both sides of the Esplanade Park as shown on the section shall be of a flowering variety. Recommended are crab apple. They shall have a maximum spacing of 25-ft. centers between trees and

25-ft. centers between pairs. They shall have a minimum canopy height of 15 ft. and a minimum caliper of 3½ in." Other controls govern streets, parking, buildings and a recreation complex. To see that all controls are honored, the planners specify a Design Review Committee, including "citizens, municipal officials, architect, local and regional planning staff."

The jurors were divided about this project. At least two of them thought it too formalistic, and perhaps too small, a plan that might work better on the grand scale from which it was taken. But the majority of the jurors found it a strong statement with an uncomplicated idea around which the town can grow. "Intelligent" and "appealing" they called it.

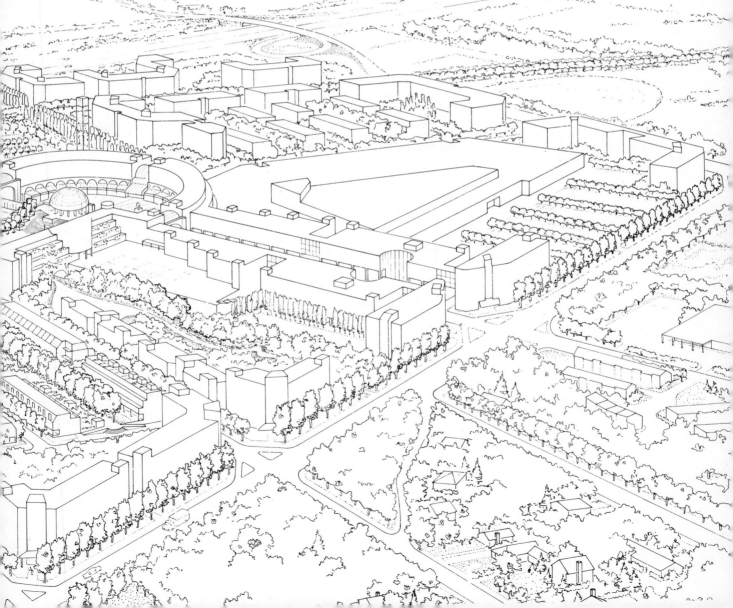

Riverdesign Dayton
Dayton, Ohio

Dayton's riverfront, unlike that of most other U.S. cities, is relatively uncluttered. It escaped the welter of railyards, factories, warehouses and junkyards that litter so many urban rivers. But at the same time it is not as much a part of the city as it could be—an asset, a place that attracts recreation and commerce. Following deadly floods in 1913, the city built dams and high levees to prevent further flood damage, and the river was pacified; but also, in part at least, it was cut off from the city, and its flow reduced to a depth not suitable for boats during the summer months.

A plan put forth by Moore Grover Harper, of Essex, Connecticut, and Lorenz and Williams (formerly Lorenz, Williams, Lively, Likens and Partners), of Dayton, perhaps ironically solves the waterfront water problem by suggesting a third dam, a low one to increase the water depth in the section of river off the central business district. When completed, the dam will back up 50 acres of water, deep enough for small boats.

In all, the plan suggests a host of activities and amenities that would make the river an important part of the city. Broad stairs, for instance, would provide safe, easy access to the river, and proper lighting (perhaps gas lights on barges that could rise and fall with the water level) would give the river appeal at night. Already in place when the study began were a bikeway and sections of a pedestrian path along the river. These were the result of an earlier plan by landscape architects Dan Kiley Associates, who in 1970 produced a "Great Miami River Study," an outgrowth of the 1967 Urban Design Conference held at the Dayton Art Institute. Kiley's plan singled out the downtown portion of the river as "the key stretch…the most complex and diverse, the most costly, the most critically important for the future of the entire river corridor plan."

The task given Moore Grover Harper and Lorenz and Williams was for detailed urban design of that 4.5-mile downtown section of the Miami. Specifically, they were charged with:

1. recognizing and using the resources of the river;
2. making sure the river stimulated future development along its banks that would preserve the river as an asset;
3. linking the river with the central business district and the adjoining neighborhoods.

In approaching point three, the planners decided it might be easier to bring the river to the town than bring the town to the river, since flood control ordinances demand that no structures be placed between the levees. So the plan proposes reopening a section of the Miami-Erie Canal that once ran where Patterson Boulevard does now. Part of the old canal bed may be usable, the planning study suggests, and the old warehouses along the boulevard can be transformed into shops, offices and residences **(1)**. Elsewhere on a six-acre site along Monument Avenue, where I-75 bridges the river, the planners suggest a 1,500 ft. canal, flowing through a proposed PUD where 330 apartments and 60,000 sq. ft.

of commercial space would face both the canal and the river (model superimposed on view of downtown Dayton **(3)**).

To garner suggestions about what the river should become, the two architectural firms turned to the people of Dayton. Most urban planning today is at least quasi-public. Committees of local residents or officers of neighborhood organizations answer planners' questions. But in Dayton the planning, to an amazing extent, was based on suggestions, thousands of them, from individuals. The planners sought these suggestions aggressively by opening a storefront office in a central downtown arcade, where they encouraged people to drop in with suggestions and where they did their planning, drawing and model work **(2)**. The suggestions were sometimes kooky (make a landing place for UFOs), sometimes conventional (make a spot to sit and watch the river) and sometimes innovative (create narrow grooved channels along each flight of steps leading to the river so that bikes can be walked down to the bike path).

But if the downtown office was static, making Daytonians come to it, the second device used by the planners was not: television. In a series of six TV shows **(4, 5)**, the planners asked viewers to phone in proposals, discussed alternatives, and asked viewers to mark ballots published in the newspaper and send them in. In this way, they tested the city's reaction to the design as it evolved.

In addition, the planners took every chance they could to meet with the community, to speak at gatherings or to open booths at special events. They mailed out questionnaires and talked with thousands of individuals. As a sort of running check on community attitudes, they formed a 50-member Citizens' Panel—50 persons recommended by neighborhood groups, institutions, businesses and agencies—whose members walked the entire 4.5 miles of the riverfront and helped define goals and issues for the study to approach.

The architect-planners published their suggestions in what they call a "Catalogue of Opportunities for a Great American River," a handsome, illustrated, easy-to-read booklet that eschews cant for a simple statement of what to do along Dayton's riverfront. Some of the suggestions are being implemented. A 3,500-ft. riverfront quay with a built-in amphitheater is under construction, funded by the State Bureau of Outdoor Recreation. A floating fountain with kiosks and a garden, sponsored by the Kiwanis Club, was launched in 1978, and a developer is working on the riverfront PUD to be built around a canal.

The architects had engineering and economic feasibility studies prepared for many of their suggestions—such as the riverside PUD and the opening of the in-town canal. In all, the plan contains 100 proposals for stairs, ramps, walkways, lighting, etc., and to see that they are implemented, an Implementation Committee was formed before the architects left town, consisting of leading Dayton businessmen and public officials, who have listed the 100 proposals by priority.

Designers: Moore Grover
Harper, architects: J.P.
Chadwick Floyd, project
manager; Charles W. Moore,
partner-in-charge. Lorenz and
Williams, Inc., architects:
Stephen J. Carter, project
manager; Leo E. Lauterbach,
partner-in-charge. Additional
design team: Robert L.
Harper, William H. Grover,
Jefferson B. Riley, Glenn W.
Arbonies, Robert E. Reed, Jr.
Graphic design: Mary Ann
Rumney, Brenda Huffman

Client: Miami Conservancy
District in cooperation with
the City of Dayton,
Montgomery County, and the
River Corridor Committee of
the Dayton Area Chamber of
Commerce

Central Washington D.C. Transportation and Civic Design Study

Designers: Joseph Passonneau and Partners: Joseph Passonneau, Laurie Olin, Jeffrey Wolf, D.L. Zolines, Victoria Steiger, Christopher Passonneau, Carla Waltz. Design: Joel Katz, Richard Saul Wurman.

Text: Joseph Passonneau, Joel Katz. Consultants: Daniel Brand, R.H. Pratt and Assoc.

1

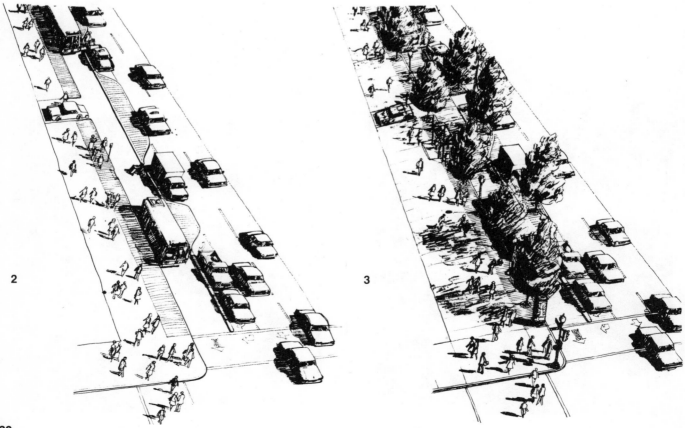

2

3

Clients: District of Columbia
Department of Transportation
and District of Columbia
Municipal Planning Office

Washington, D.C. was laid out in 1791 for a transportation system of horses and carts. Though its avenues are grand, they are obviously taxed by the automobile. In the years since the motor car overtook the horse and trolley, sacrifices have been made in its behalf: sidewalks narrowed, trees removed and limits of pollution reached. Washington is a particularly noisome example of automobile dominance. According to the report "Central Washington, D.C. Transportation and Civic Design Study": "Over 75,000 autos enter the downtown during rush hour, more than twice as many as enter the Chicago Loop or downtown Los Angeles, slightly more cars than enter downtown New York and probably more cars than enter any other central city in the world." Weekdays, roads leading into Washington are jammed by 6:30 a.m.

Two projects are underway which may restore Washington's streets to their intended elegance and make travel on them a good deal easier. The first project is the Metro subway, whose initial stops opened in 1976. The second is the redesign of the city's streets. To an extent the success of Metro, which will need street access to and from its stations, depends on unclogged streets, and in the "Transportation and Civic Design Study," Washington has a plan for freeing them, little by little, at manageable expense.

The study's recommendations are uncomplicated. They call for elimination of as much street parking as possible, offering parking space instead in garages, where rates would favor short-term stays. These rates would, in other words, favor shoppers rather than commuters, who, because of parking costs, will find it cheaper to take subway or bus. The space gained on streets by eliminating lines of parked cars would either be converted to bus lanes, so that buses could run freely without snarling traffic and keeping riders waiting, or converted to extended sidewalks with space for kiosks and trees. Lots of trees (see plan and **(3)**). Trees protected from damage. Cities have traditionally had lots of street trees, the study reminds us. But (at least in Washington) many of these trees became casualties of auto pollution and auto-forced street widening. To go with its recommended changes, the study suggests varied street paving with one type for sidewalks, another for streets, and yet a third as a surface for building entrance, crosswalk, curb, tree root protection or seating area. Basic to the plan is a strip between sidewalk and street, planted with trees perhaps, but with occasional "lay-byes" where trucks could pull out of traffic to unload, or taxis take on passengers **(1)**. Moreover, exclusive lanes for trucks, carpools or taxis with multiple fares **(2)** should be added, says the study, and, where possible, exclusive bicycle lanes.

What would these changes cost? According to the study, an estimated $50,000 to $100,000 per 100 ft. in 1976 dollars. This figure is more than American cities currently spend on their streets, but less than European cities do. In any case, the price would be repaid by making Washington, or any city which followed the suggestions, quieter, prettier and easier to move around in.

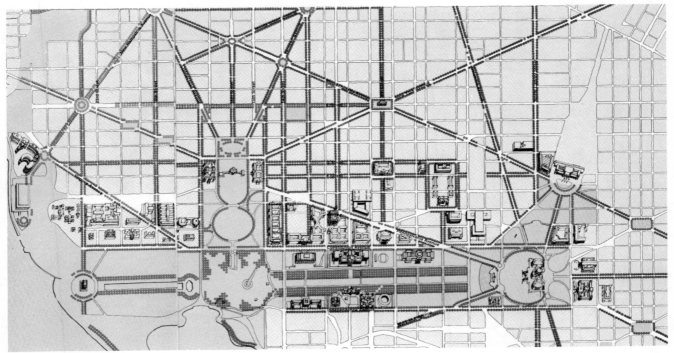

Neighborhood Development

Dundas/Sherbourne Infill Housing,
Toronto, Ontario, Canada

Designers: A. J. Diamond and Barton Myers, architects: Barton Myers, designer. Barton Myers Assoc., implementation: David W. Oleson, project architect.

The neighborhood committee worried more about what the twin 24-story towers planned for Toronto's Dundas/Sherbourne block would do to the low- and middle-income pensioners who lived there, than about the necessary destruction of the 19th-century houses they lived in. The twin towers would house only families and individuals with higher income, and the neighborhood residents would be forced to move, the committee feared. But their bulldog opposition led the builder to give up his plans and sell his land. He sold it to the city, which took over the project. Finding the city more tractable, the neighborhood committee (the South of Carlton Area Working Committee) persuaded it to retain the old houses and, by adding new low-rise infill housing, to increase the neighborhood's density without destroying its character or displacing its residents.

The oldest of the houses on Sherbourne's 200 block went up in about 1856 and is of vibrantly patterned red and white brick. The neighborhood's variety is diffuse. There are houses representing styles that were popular (sometimes only in Toronto) in each decade of the late 19th century and in the first decade of the 20th. There is a frame house from the late 1860s with a brick veneer attached in the 1890s. Two houses have swelling bow fronts, slated mansard roofs and strong cable moldings around most openings. There is a double house representing the Georgian row houses common in Toronto in the late 1840s and '50s. The street was and is distinctive in its grand scale.

The city-built infill housing, financed by Canadian Federal N. H. A. funds and by Ontario rent-supplement programs, is secured by a 50-year, eight percent mortgage, reduced by a ten percent forgiveness. This cooperation among federal, provincial and city governments set a pattern followed several times since in Toronto.

About 75 percent of the Dundas/Sherbourne infill housing

Client: City of Toronto
Non-Profit Housing Corp.:
Robert Millward, director

is earmarked for low-income individuals and families, and to ensure that the neighborhood continue to be home for a range of different-sized families, the housing offers a mixture of apartment sizes. These include about 100 single rooms, 228 one-bedroom apartments and 53 units of from two to five bedrooms. In this way, the committee hoped to provide for all — roomers, senior citizens, couples, and couples with children. At the same time, the committee and the city went to some length to ensure everyone a modicum of privacy. Drawing on the advice of Dr. William Michelson, a University of Toronto sociologist, the architects

1. arranged private entrances, where possible, directly off the street;

2. placed children's play areas so that mothers, working in their apartments, can keep an eye on the kids;

3. created buffers between the children and the other residents;

4. offered direct access from ground-floor apartments **(1)** to private open space;

5. clearly defined the walkways and open spaces leading to individual apartments as private or semiprivate;

6. created space for a day-care center adjacent to one of the play areas.

But perhaps most important, the architects blended the new buildings with the texture of the neighborhood, using lots of brick and holding the scale to that of the old houses **(2)**. Though obvious, the new buildings do not dominate or jar, and they relate invitingly to the neighborhood's open spaces and to the older houses **(3,4)**. The new buildings are as high as seven stories and no lower than five, but their upper stories step back, breaking up what might have become barrier-like facades. Angles and indentations abound; so do expanses of glass and balcony undulations.

Glencoe Place Public Improvements
Cincinnati, Ohio

Designers: City of Cincinnati, Office of Architecture and Urban Design: Ronald B. Kull, principal architect and urban designer; Robert Richardson, senior architect and urban designer; W. Michael Pachan, Carl Jahnes, architects. Mt. Auburn Good Housing Foundation, housing rehabilitation: A. Vernon Friason, director; Carl Westmoreland, president; Goetzman and Follmer, architects

The buildings in Glencoe, just below Auburn Avenue, the backbone of Mt. Auburn, the hilltop suburb of Cincinnati, originally went up as a pocket of low-income housing in the late 1800s to house factory workers. Bounded by the hills of Inwood Park to the northwest and Christ Hospital to the south (see area plan), it decayed in recent years until finally its buildings stood vacant and vandalized. Glencoe became known as "the hole" of Mt. Auburn. But three or four years ago, Carl Westmoreland, energetic president of the nonprofit Mt. Auburn Good Housing Foundation, Inc., went to the Cincinnati Office of Architecture and Urban Design, asking for a plan that might solve Glencoe's problems. Not only did the city come up with a plan to give the area new life but it also funded the plan's suggested public improvements. So far, the city has channeled close to a million dollars in Federal NDP and city money into lighting, parking, playgrounds and other amenities, and the Good Housing Foundation has renovated 290 housing units.

Inherent in the plan was the belief that the neighborhood's character could be changed if housing restoration went hand-in-hand with beautification of the surroundings. So, while the Good Housing Foundation, with private funds, fixed up the old brick row houses, restoring their facades and retaining their historical character, the city went to work on the neighborhood beyond the houses.

Selected Glencoe houses were bought by the city and were removed, in order to reduce the area's poverty of light and air by reducing the building density, and to make way for playgrounds and parking. Breezes have more chance of getting to the restored apartments now, and children can play in any of three neighborhood playgrounds **(1)** that have old-fashioned play equipment (horseshoe pits, climbing poles, sliding tubes and tire swings).

There is shaded seating for adults. And there is more elegant seating in View Court, a dead-end street which was closed to vehicles and made into a courtyard (see plan). Throughout Glencoe, the city installed handsome light fixtures, removing utility poles and burying wires. Along the new sidewalks, trees were planted; connecting two of the recreation areas is a walkway between rows of rear courtyards **(2)**.

Glencoe now has housing in 90 low-to-middle-income family units with 49 parking spaces for workers at nearby Christ Hospital and at the University of Cincinnati. And these families are no longer faced with the possibility of having to leave the neighborhood.

1

Client: City of Cincinnati, William V. Donaldson, city manager. Department of Development: Nell Surber, director; Frank Taylor, assistant director; Ralph Bolton, development officer.

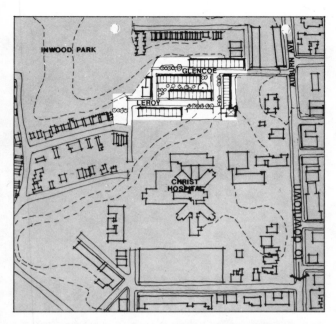

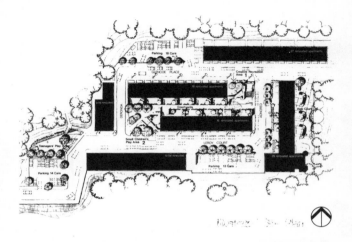

Metro North Plaza
New York, N.Y.

Designers: Conklin and Rossant, architects and planners: Arthur Wexler, project manager for housing; Robert C. McMillan, project manager for school

Clients: New York State Urban Development Corporation; New York City Educational Construction Fund; Sovereign/Quest, division of Titan Corporation

Instead of looking over the East River at 101st Street in Manhattan, the Metro North Riverview Houses eschew their name and location to focus on the streets around them (see site plan). On the streets is where the life of this east Harlem community is, and the Metro North Association, the community group active in planning this new low- and middle-income housing with architects Conklin and Rossant and the New York State Urban Development Corporation, wanted residents at Metro North to be part of that life. Too much of the city's highrise cruciform housing, set back on tracts of open land, isolate the tenants and encourage crime, the association argued. Instead, the association wanted to offer residents protection by bringing the street into the project. Architects Conklin and Rossant accomplished this by forming the 761 housing units, which are tiered, in buildings rising to 15 stories at their highest point, around three interior courtyards, connected by a single walkway-spine **(1)** to First Avenue.

At the edge of the complex facing the river are a parking structure for 285 cars and an elementary school for 1,400 students **(2)**. P-50 is one of the first open classroom schools in Manhattan and in the same building is a new home for the Harlem School of Performing Arts, a special school which helps students learn through the excitement of performing.

Students reach the school and tenants their apartments by entering Metro North Riverside Houses on the walkway-spine leading from First Avenue. Off this walkway tenants turn to enter semi-private courtyards, in which are the apartment building entrances. "We have a sort of hierarchy of public and private uses," says architect William Conklin. "Retail shops in Metro North's first level line First Avenue and the corners turning into the main entrance walk. People enter the project past these shops, moving into the mall, through the courtyards into their own buildings and their own elevators."

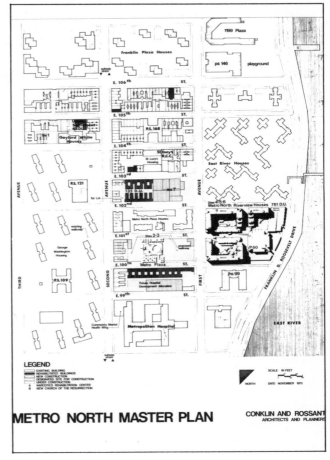

METRO NORTH MASTER PLAN   CONKLIN AND ROSSANT ARCHITECTS AND PLANNERS

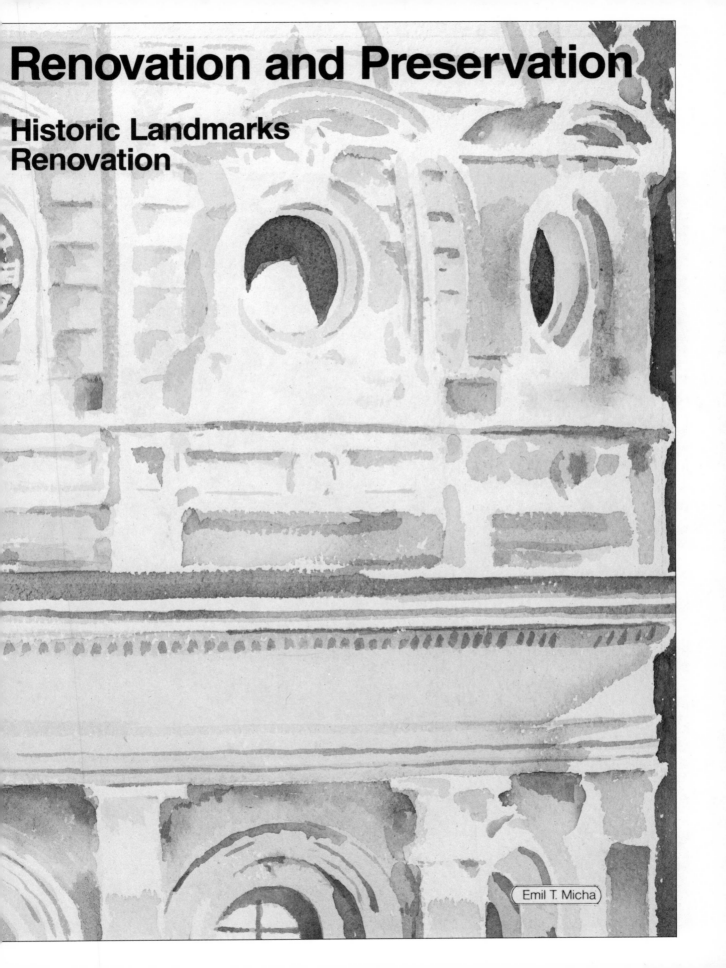

Renovation and Preservation

Historic Landmarks
Renovation

Emil T. Micha

**City of Charleston
Preservation Effort:
College of Charleston
Campus/Market Square/
Spoleto Festival U.S.A.**
Charleston, S.C.

Designers: For College of Charleston, Edward Pinckney Assoc. Ltd., landscape architects and planners: James K. Tiller III, project manager. For Market Square, Harold Adler, architect. Kamstra-Dickerson Assoc. Inc., associate architects. Edward Pinckney Assoc. Ltd., landscape consultant. Joe Sonderman Design Inc., design consultants. For Spoleto, Spoleto Festival Inc.

Clients: For College of Charleston, Theodore S. Stern, president, and State of South Carolina. For Market Square, Save Charleston Partnership: William E. Murray, Harold Adler.

Charleston was once one of the U. S.'s major ports. Its old homes are among the grandest in the nation, well preserved, lovingly cared for, with gardens that make even the most casual visitor long to tarry. But other parts of this city of 70,000 experienced decay, and it is only recently that a foresighted citizenry started to remold Charleston. Part of this effort intends to make people more aware of the city's charms. Another part of the effort is an outright wooing of tourists and conventioneers. And more visitors mean greater strain on city resources. This strain is being eased by planning.

One of the events that is awakening tourist interest in Charleston is the **Spoleto Festival U. S. A.** Twenty-one years ago, composer Gian-Carlo Menotti established an arts festival in Spoleto, Italy. He had always wanted to add an American equivalent, and in 1977 he did. In 12 days that year, more than 150 performing events took place in Charleston parks, streets, theaters, churches and auditoriums. Menotti chose Charleston because it had an outstanding range of performing facilities and because, like Spoleto, the city is itself a work of art. Now held yearly in the late spring, Spoleto Festival U. S. A. brings to Charleston opera, theater, dance, film, chamber music, jazz. A good deal of all this is performed outdoors in public spaces. In addition, there are what the promoters call mini-festivals. These, held mostly in parks and other public spaces, are performances by storytellers, puppeteers, mimes, with music and crafts displays and instant theater. Many of these mini-festivals involve the spectators in the performances, and more than that, they involve the spectators in the public spaces, making people aware of the spaces and their vitality in a way that lingers when the festival is over for the year.

Along with the renewed awareness of the city has come the need to accommodate crowds of tourists. (Many Charleston citizens open their homes to guests during the festival. But not everyone likes the tourists. They strain city facilities. More horse-drawn carriages to take tourists around town, for instance, has meant more manure on the streets, leading to a city ordinance requiring horse diapers on each horse.) To relieve tourist pressure on downtown Charleston, Market Square was developed as a focus of downtown browsing, shopping and snacking.

Market Square grew out of the Save Charleston Foundation's fight to stop a high-rise development in the shadow of the city's most revered landmark, St. Philip's Church. Privately organized, the Foundation raised more than $500,000 in 49 states and 13 foreign countries to help buy the property. By retaining three structures, building new ones no higher than 50 ft. and turning historic Lodge Alley into a pedestrian thoroughfare, the new developers, the Save Charleston Partnership, turned the area into a bustling one of markets, restaurants and small family-operated shops. Total investment has been more than $1.5 million and value of the improved area is an estimated $4 million.

The area has seen 27 new businesses open, which compete successfully with out-of-town shopping centers. Moreover, Market Square has become, as it was supposed to, the focus for the city's street life. Daily, people wander the sidewalks there, looking at crafts, displays, listening to outdoor concerts, watching each other. Many of the city's professional people lunch there each noon **(1, 2)**. In the area's center, Market Square, a fountain now spouts **(3)**, reassembled from pieces found lying in weeds behind the city's park maintenance department. This may make the area sound as if it is pieced together from hand-me-down buildings and accoutrements, but the point is: it works. It is a shopping, strolling and snacking area that pulls people in, people who had no other place to congregate.

In the center of the city, the **College of Charleston**, founded in 1770, now part of the South Carolina State System of Higher Education, sits on ten blocks of land interlaced with historic residences. Under the leadership of Theodore Stern, a nephew of Robert Moses, the college's growth has blended with the area, welding it together and, not incidentally, sparking restoration of some of the older homes. All the college's new buildings and landscaping details, such as walks, walls and planting-borders, are of warm-toned brick **(4)**, similar in color and texture to the old Charleston brick seen everywhere in the city, in garden walls and walks and in the houses themselves. The college buildings are laced together with walks and gardens **(5)** that mirror those in the rest of the city and preserve its intimate grandeur.

**Warehouse District
Movement: Cleveland
Warehouse District
Plan 1977 and SoHo,
New York City**

Designers: For Cleveland,
William A. Gould and Assoc.,
architects and city planners:
William A. Gould, principal;
Ronald P. Gronowski,
associate and project
director; William O. Lindow,
Stanley E. Martin, Karen E.
Jewell, Rosemary G.
Oldenburg, project team

Client: Cleveland Landmarks
Commission: John D.
Cimperman, director

During the '70s, the warehouse-loft movement spread across the country from New York to Chicago, St. Louis, Kansas City, Denver and San Francisco, and to Baltimore, Minneapolis, New Orleans and Los Angeles. For the most part there is a pattern to the movement, though, as the decade wanes, the pattern is becoming diffuse, infiltrated by imitation and innovation, and is no longer so easy to define. In its pure form it works something like this. Warehouse or light manufacturing space lies vacant. The raccoon-skinning factory, the cannery or the cotton importer has gone out of business and the building stands, structurally sound, but without any takers for its original use. Looking for large swatches of work space, which they can also live in, artists seek out these older lofts, clean out the debris, add some pipes for kitchens, and move in at low rents. Owners are glad to find a use, any use, for their buildings and to have someone there to look after them. If enough artists arrive in an area, it becomes chic. Boutiques, restaurants, galleries spring up, and so do rents. Developers move in, renovate other loft spaces and rent them for rates the artists cannot afford. The artists move on, looking once again for cheap, unadulterated space.

The story of artists and inexpensive work space goes back, of course, for centuries. This is merely our present decade's version of it. A spate of warehouse conversion is passing across the country. In New York City's SoHo district, which pioneered the current pattern, lofts have become so fashionable that legitimate, profitable manufacturing is being forced out. The buildings are now more valuable converted to residences.

In Cleveland, the pattern will be somewhat different. Cleveland's warehouse district **(3)** lies along the shores of Lake Erie, between the lakefront Municipal Stadium and the Terminal Tower, between the industrial valley of the Cuyahoga River and the government center. Comprising some 40 acres, the district has a concentration of 19th-century commercial buildings, many of them historically and architecturally significant. Six of its buildings are in the National Register of Historic Places, and the Cleveland Landmarks Commission has singled out 34 for special attention. In recent years the pressures of the warehouse district have come from a demand for parking to support surrounding activities. Many of the district's buildings have been demolished, others lost to fires. And parking lots have taken their place. The area supports 4,700 unrestricted parking spaces, and the Greater Cleveland Growth Association estimates a long-term demand for 8,000.

To show how the area's character can be established and preserved is the purpose of the Cleveland Warehouse District Plan, made possible in part by a grant from the National Endowment for the Arts (City Options program), and in part by backing from the Cleveland Landmarks Commission. The plan suggests a program of reuse of existing real estate and the addition of new structures.

William A. Gould and Associates, who prepared the plan, suggest a pattern of mixed uses within the area. Where possible, they envision buildings housing ground-floor retail space, mid-level parking, and on the upper floors, office or residential space **(2)**. They further suggest turning some of the vacant sites into mini-parks and engaging city government in a program of street improvement to go with private rehabilitation of buildings.

The plan suggests the possibility of converting some warehouse space into residential lofts. But the suggestion is muted. While loft conversions have been highly successful in New York, Chicago and other major cities, Cleveland's circumstances are special. Cleveland does not have a large artists' community to convert and live in loft space. As Jim Stratton notes in his excellent book on lofts, *Pioneering in the Urban Wilderness,* there are probably more Cleveland artists in New York than there are in Cleveland. "There may be more artists *from* Ohio," he writes, "than *in* Ohio."

But loft space can appeal to others besides artists. And Cleveland may be able to skip the first phase of the warehouse conversion pattern, bypassing artists and their quest for inexpensive loft space, to encourage loft habitation by professional urban couples, lawyers, accountants, doctors, bankers and persons returning to the city from the suburbs.

The plan suggests tax incentives for renovation in the warehouse district, incentives which will only come once both government and citizens are aware of the district's history and architecture.

Perhaps the most important outgrowth of the Cleveland Warehouse District Plan is a new city procedure used in applying for building permits and appeals for historic buildings. Worked out by the Board of Building Standards and Appeals and by the Cleveland Landmarks Commission, the procedure tries to simplify the red tape of rehabilitation.

Also, the Landmarks Commission is taking steps to have the area designated an Historic District.

Some renovation is already completed:

• A former warehouse is now the Happy Apple, a melange of bars, shops, restaurants and a disco.

Other rehabilitation is under way:

• A warehouse is being converted by a local advertising firm to house commercial shops and loft apartments.

Moreover, projects for new building are under way:

• Higbees department store put Settlers Landing at the district's southwest corner, six and a half acres of restaurants, shops, offices (150,000 sq. ft.) and entertainment facilities. A first phase saw the renovation of the Western Reserve Building **(1)**.

• A mixed-use office complex was recently announced for a site within the district.

Essential for success of the district, warns the plan, is coordination of private and public groups. Public agencies must make building codes flexible enough so that rehabilitation is not stifled, and must help provide public services. Private groups must become aware of the benefits of financial aid to private developers within the district, and citizens in the area must form a local, non-profit development corporation, which can secure money and ease the way through the bureaucracy for people who live in and want to change the area—while retaining its character.

1

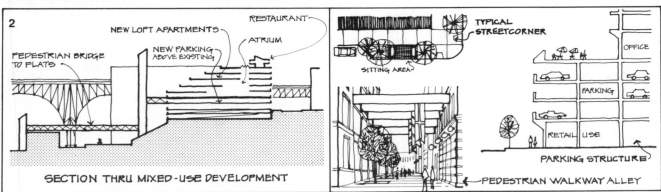

2

PEDESTRIAN BRIDGE TO FLATS

NEW LOFT APARTMENTS

NEW PARKING ABOVE EXISTING

ATRIUM

RESTAURANT

SECTION THRU MIXED-USE DEVELOPMENT

TYPICAL STREETCORNER

SITTING AREA

OFFICE

PARKING

RETAIL USE

PARKING STRUCTURE

PEDESTRIAN WALKWAY ALLEY

3

Laclede's Landing—
Urban Design Guideline
St. Louis, Mo.

Designers: Hellmuth, Obata and Kassabaum, Inc., architects, engineers, planners: Neil Porterfield, principal; Terry Harkness, designer.

Client: Laclede's Landing Redevelopment Corporation: Thomas Purcell, executive director.

Laclede's Landing is historic. There is little doubt about it. Several of the buildings there are the city's best examples of 19th-century cast-iron architecture **(1)**; more than 30 buildings (there are 35 in all) date from the 1800s, and the street pattern is that of the original city that grew up around the French trading post established in 1764. Most of the other original parts of the city have been bulldozed away. South of Laclede's Landing on cleared land is Gateway Arch. But protected by Eads Bridge to the south, by Martin Luther King Bridge to the north and to the west by the Mark Twain Expressway, the Landing was spared **(2)**. St. Louis had time to become aware of the Landing's historic importance and its current potential.

In 1966, the city gave Laclede's Landing access to urban renewal and restoration money. The arrangement was that a city-approved redevelopment corporation would get property-tax abatement and have the backing of the city's eminent-domain powers for work in the area. But nothing happened. Single developers ran aground on the economic shoals of those years. Nothing continued to happen until 1974, when a group of the Landing's property-owners and businessmen, spurred by designer Dwight Reum, formed a steering committee to do something about local problems, such as harassment by building inspectors and the deafness of banks who were asked for improvement funds. Some renovation, done by individuals, got publicity, and by the end of 1975 the committee had formed the Laclede's Landing Redevelopment Corporation. Half its stockholders are building owners, the other half civic groups and banks. Owners renovate their buildings themselves rather than rely on a single outside developer. Working through the LLDC, they share the advantages of the city's tax abatement and eminent-domain laws, and perhaps just as important, they have behind them the city's commitment to smooth the way for the area's renovation. Because many single owners are doing work, the amounts of cash raised are many and small; the risk is spread and so is the work.

But because so many are involved, the need for design guidelines became imperative. Owners needed a guide they could refer to as they renovated their buildings, a set of rules to ensure the quality of redevelopment and the preservation of the area's history. The Urban Design Guidelines, worked out by Hellmuth, Obata and Kassabaum, Inc., set three major goals:

1. To preserve and rehabilitate the historically significant structures.

2. To preserve the basic street patterns.

3. To preserve the area's unique character by establishing design standards for rehabilitation, new construction, maintenance and occupancy of all the area's properties.

These guidelines represent a refinement and interpretation of the Laclede's Landing Development Plan, adopted by St. Louis in 1975. Choice of the word "guidelines," state Hellmuth, Obata and Kassabaum, "was made with particular care. It is based upon the recognition that rigid controls or predetermined rules do more harm than good when applied to complex renewal undertakings of this nature. The ultimate environmental quality must be determined by factors in addition to this document. These include encouragement of capable design professionals and application of a design review function."

Set forth in a 136-page looseleaf book, the guidelines are to be used by anyone working in the area: private building owners, the city, utility companies, private outside developers, investors and the LLRC.

Here is a sampling:

• "All service delivery, refuse and storage receptacles for private use will be located inside the existing or new buildings."

• "Phased removal of all on-street parking is recommended."

• "Major new buildings taller than 102 ft. above their block shall have a breakline equal to the highest average level of existing buildings in adjacent blocks." The idea is to preserve sightlines on the sloping site.

• "All street curbing shall be granite wherever feasible."

• "All new sidewalks shall be brick (red, common) and shall be placed in a continuous basket-weave pattern."

• "All lighting shall incorporate a traditional pole with a contemporary fixture." (3)

Further edicts are set for tree planting, signage and banners. And specific edicts are issued for specific blocks on the Landing.

So far the guidelines have eased the redevelopment. Work is completed on the Landing's streets and on two major buildings. Eight other buildings are in the design or construction stages.

3

Cobble Hill Towers
Brooklyn, N.Y.

Designers: Maitland/
Strauss/Behr, architects.
Robert Silman Assoc.,
structural consultants.
George Langer, mechanical
consultants. John Mee, Inc.,
contractor.

None of the residents wanted to leave. The location in Brooklyn's Cobble Hill section (one of New York City's landmark districts) suited them, and so did the rents in their century-old buildings. Cobble Hill Towers, a nine-building complex, went up in 1876-79, one of the nation's first housing projects, paid for by a local philanthropist. Its renovation is not being undertaken by an individual, but by a consortium of city, state, federal and private investment. The buildings had reached a point where their deterioration, which had moved relatively slowly for 100 years, was being hastened by vandalism. Frank Farella, who owns the project, thinks its refurbishing will stem the vandalism; indeed, his reasoning has support. Tenants have a new pride in their apartments. And

many have expressed their desire to maintain the renovated buildings. All seem happy to have their surroundings fixed up, at no cost to themselves, and to be able to stay in the renovated apartments without a rent increase. (Part of the complicated financial arrangement is a HUD rent subsidy program—Section 8.) Renovated apartments rent for about $65 a room. Apartment size is increased in the renovated building layouts, which offer more than 200 apartments.

Cobble Hill Towers are unlike a contemporary development in many ways. Residents climb to apartment floors through exterior stair towers. These, with arched openings facing the street, are set off by flanking columns of recessed balconies with wrought-iron balustrades **(1, 3)**. At the top,

Clients: Cobble Hill View
Towers, Inc.: Frank Farella,
president. New York City
Department of Housing
Preservation and
Development: Nathan
Leventhal, commissioner.
Chemical Bank.
Independence Savings Bank.

beneath the building's cornice, is some handsome brick corbeling **(2)**.

To support the restoration, Farella and architects Maitland/Strauss/Behr put together a complex financing package. A matching grant of $200,000 under the 1966 Historic Preservation Act, appropriated by the New York State Park and Recreation Commission, ensured accurate restoration of the buildings' facades. A mortage for the work came from the New York City Participation Loan program, set up to encourage joint private and municipal rehabilitation of city neighborhoods. Under this program, the city's Office of Rehabilitation and Neighborhood Development channeled federal Community Development funds into the project. The other half of the $3.7-million mortgage was financed conventionally by Brooklyn's Independence Savings Bank. Its commitment is for 25 years at nine-and-a-half percent. The city's half is being repaid with one percent interest, which brings the average interest to less than five percent.

The project benefits further from the city's J-51 program of tax abatement. Established in 1955, J-51 exempts a building from increased tax assessment for 12 years after the improvements are made. In addition, Cobble Hill Towers, registered as a national landmark, was eligible for accelerated five-year depreciation.

3

**Baltimore City Hall and
Plaza Restoration**
Baltimore, Md.

Designers: Architectural
Heritage-Baltimore, Inc.,
architects: Thomas Amsler,
Charles Hagenah, Kenneth
MacLean/Meyers, D'Aleo and
Patton, Inc., associated
architects

Under the leadership of Mayor William Donald Schaefer, Baltimore is becoming keenly aware of its architectural heritage and is working to preserve it. The latest evidence of this awareness is the renovation of the 100-year-old City Hall. Built in 1875 in the Second Empire style popular in France from about 1850 to 1870, by architect George Frederick, who was then only 25, the structure never had a thorough overhaul. Its electrical system had been added to, piecemeal, and its heating system shored up occasionally. But the dirt had accumulated beyond sanction, and decay was more than incidental. When, in 1959, a 15-pound piece of rusted decoration fell from the dome into the Board of

Estimate room, it was taken as an omen; but it was not until 1974 that a plan to stem the decay jelled. In that year Mayor Schaefer proposed putting an $8-million bond issue on the ballot to help pay for the $9.8-million renovation suggested by the City Planning Commission. A comparable new building, architects estimated, would cost $14.4 million. A decisive 61 percent of Baltimore voters approved the bonds and work went ahead.

The new building plans offered almost twice as much usable space while restoring the grand features of the old building. Over the years the central rotunda, beneath a stained glass oculus in the dome, became cluttered with

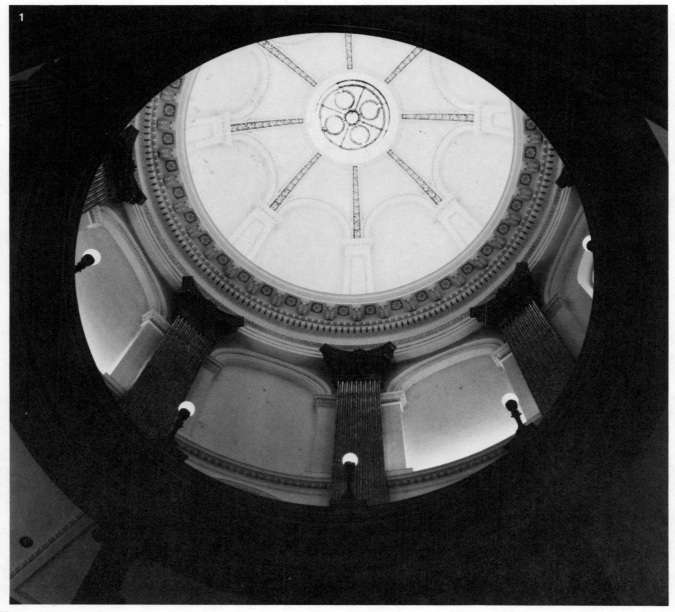

Clients: City of Baltimore: William Donald Schaefer, mayor; Baltimore City Department of Planning: Larry Reich, director; Arthur Valk, project planner; Department of Public Works: Edward Oppel, construction manager; Baltimore Commission for Historical and Architectural Preservation: Barbara Hoff, executive director

storage. The clutter gone, the rotunda and its rings of marble balustraded balconies became part of the building's circulation; people pass through the rotunda on their way from the main entrance to the elevators. With the stained glass cleaned of a century of grime (1) and the inlaid marble floor polished, the rotunda is elegant once again. Courtyards on either side of it, also cleared of storage, are once again open space. Given skylights (2), they serve as lobbies; offices and corridors on four floors now overlook them through arched windows and from balconies (3).

To provide added office space, the architects cleared the basement, fitting offices among its arched brick vaults and bearing walls (4). Then, in the 19-ft. vertical spans between the second and third floors, they added a mezzanine, inserting another between the third and fourth floors. Some of the larger, fine old spaces, such as the mayor's reception room (6) with its brass and crystal chandeliers, its mahogany shutters, its brass-capitaled scagliola pilasters and its Victorian furnishings, were restored. So was the City Council Chamber (5) and the Board of Estimate Room. In the BOE Room now hang portraits of former Baltimore mayors, and elsewhere in the building hang photo blowups of the city and its historic events, paid for by the city's one-percent-for-art law.

Outside, workmen removed the dome's cast-iron panels, cleaned them, eliminating rust, recasting some plates, then rebolting and painting them **(7)**.

Cleaned and refurbished, the City Hall **(8)** stands out as what it is: the centerpiece of Baltimore's municipal district. In its vicinity are a cluster of significant new and old buildings — I. M. Pei's pentagonal 30-story World Trade Center, the Inner Harbor campus of the Community College of Baltimore, the old Central Post Office (rehabilitated for city offices) and the old Federal Court House. Eventually, these buildings will be linked by a mall, for which City Hall will be the anchor. Because of a fire in 1904, which burned 140 acres of downtown Baltimore before stopping just short of City Hall, the land across the street has been a plaza for more than half a century. During restoration work Holliday Street, in front of City Hall, was closed and the space between street and building turned into another plaza, linked to War Memorial Plaza by extending the double rows of trees that flank it. A third row of trees will give shade to more benches.

7

8

William R. Cobb, of the architectural office of Lord and Burnham, is credited with the design of the Bronx Botanical Garden Conservatory. With its central rotunda, or Palm House **(1)**, and its ten other connected greenhouses, arranged in a C-shape (see plan), the Conservatory houses close to an acre of plants (42,000 sq. ft.). It went up between 1899 and 1902 at the tail end of the era of the great glass-enclosed space. It has overtones of the Royal Botanical Gardens at Kew, whose Palm House opened in 1847, and, of course, of Sir Joseph Paxton's Crystal Palace, built for London's Great Exhibition of 1851 and recycled the following year as a winter garden at Sydenham. Today, there is a resurgence of these public spaces under glass.

This particular one works for several reasons. It serves as a symbol of rebirth in its neighborhood. That area of the Bronx is decaying. In fact, the Conservatory was perhaps the most decayed and vandalized of nearby structures. By 1970 there seemed little else to do but pull the building down. On its opening in 1901 it had been called "one of the most elegant buildings in the world." And it would have come down had it not been for a private donation of $5 million. It works, too, because it brings a world of plants to city dwellers who can go for months without seeing a tree. At the Conservatory, New Yorkers can touch a plant, stand in air that smells of moist earth and flowers. There is something for everyone. Plants collected and arranged by horticulturist Carlton Lees will offer clouds of blooms as well as examples of hybrid genealogy. A "please touch" garden is meant to acquaint city youngsters with the way vegetables look and feel while still growing, before they reach supermarket bins. There are also examples of plant-training techniques: topiary, bansai, espalier.

Architect Edward Larrabee Barnes has meandering paths, with special paving (desert-like rock in the American desert house, for instance) winding through the wings linking the larger corner pavilions. In these more formal pavilions are specialized displays, which can be seen from viewing platforms. In one pavilion a skywalk crosses above a pool and a mountain setting of ferns. Outside, the buildings have been returned to nearly their original condition. The main entrance, "modernized" in 1953, is restored to the way it looked in old drawings and photographs. Often the materials used are the same as the original ones — limestone, steel, wrought iron. Sometimes they are more contemporary, such as applied ornament cast from aluminum. Reconstructed is a wooden condensation-gutter system, and tucked away inside the glass spaces is contemporary mechanical equipment for humidity and temperature control.

New classroom facilities above the vegetable garden galleries offer space for botany workshops and art classes. Beneath the Conservatory, linking two of its remote pavilions, is a newly-dug tunnel lined with corrugated steel. Here, mushrooms and other fungi breed and grow.

New York Botanical Garden Conservatory
Bronx, N.Y.

Designers: Edward Larrabee Barnes, architects: Alistair Bevington, Percy K. Keck, associates. Kiley, Tyndall, Walker, landscape architects: Peter Ker Walker, partner-in-charge. Carlton B. Lees, New York Botanical Garden exhibition designer

Client: New York Botanical Garden: Carlton B. Lees, senior vice president

History Corner Reconstruction, Stanford University
Stanford, Ca.

Designers: Stone, Marraccini and Patterson, architects. Esherick Homsey Dodge and Davis, architects. Richard Vignolo, landscape architect

Client: Leland Stanford Jr. University

Stanford University was laid out starting in 1887 in the midst of 8,000 acres of grassland and foothills on the San Francisco peninsula. Its plan was the work of Frederic Law Olmsted, who, with the consent and constraint of his client, Leland Stanford, Sr., organized the university buildings in two concentric quadrangles, a plan more derivative of architecture in Syria, Greece, Italy and Spain than of Western Europe. This arrangement, the two men felt, suited the California climate and locale—and the architecture by Charles Alberton Coolidge, who, with two partners, had just taken over the practice of the late Henry Hobson Richardson. Richardson's Romanesque style proved remarkably well-suited to the quadrangles, cloisters, landscaped courts and gardens, sandstone walls and multiplaned red tile roofs of the resulting university. Historians linked the architecture to Granada's Alhambra of the 14th century, but also to that of fifth- and sixth-century Byzantine churches and to the Romanesque period in France.

As the campus grew during the 20th century, it spread beyond the original quadrangles, through the 8,000 acres. It would have been possible to replace the old inner buildings or to abandon them and to use as the campus only what had grown beyond them. But to abandon them would be to abandon what Lewis Mumford once called the "compactness, concentration and unity" of Olmsted's plan.

The inner courtyard has 12 one-story buildings and a Memorial Church, arranged around a huge rectangular courtyard. Surrounding all this is the outer quadrangle of one- to four-story buildings. The quadrangles stand much as they originally did, though one of the inner quad buildings has a second story, added in 1944 as offices for the university president.

Restoration costs are running up to 20 percent more than

new construction, but the university thinks it a small price to pay for retention of the old campus core. Work is progressing on the outer quad buildings first. Three are completed, two now being restored and three more in planning stages. Funding for these renovations, which are now costing about $4 to $5 million per building, comes from combinations of donations, operating funds, reserves and borrowing. The most recent renovation, scheduled for completion in mid-1979, is the northeast corner of the outer quad, the History Corner. Because the faculty using the building needs no additional space, it is possible to save both interior and exterior. But even so, the renovation process here, as elsewhere at Stanford, is arduous.

History Corner, like other quad buildings, is what one engineer calls "a pile of bricks and stone which somehow has to be tied together and kept from falling apart during an earthquake"...an unreinforced brick structure with sandstone facing. Using the second-story wooden floor as a form support for a new concrete slab floor, the designers, once the slab is set, then will brace the walls above the second floor with a framework of steel reinforcing rods, and remove the wooden floors and roof. Outer walls will be reinforced with gunite concrete and braced with steel rods and the roof replaced with one of fireproofed steel frame, metal decking and concrete fill.

Inside, the building will not be exactly the same as it was but will still retain the building's "familiar form and personality." Classrooms are designed to be convertible to offices, meaning that the duct-work and electric wiring will be arranged accordingly. But the old interiors' wood wainscots, wooden door frames and trim and natural finish hardwood doors are all being retained and used. So are the wrought steel handrail from the original interior stairs.

In 1735, John Peter Zenger was arrested on what is now the site of St. Paul's Church in Mt. Vernon, N.Y., Town of Eastchester, just north of New York City's Borough of the Bronx. Zenger, editor of the *Weekly Journal*, had printed some unkind things about the British governor of New York and was put on trial. Zenger's acquittal gave the idea of freedom of the press a legal foothold in the colonies. Almost 30 years later, by coincidence, a church went up on the site, and though it has sheltered an Episcopalian congregation for more than 200 years, it has seen other uses. For a while it served as a courthouse, where Alexander Hamilton argued points of law. And for a time during the Revolutionary War, it was a hospital.

A handsome, simple brick church, it suffered neglect in recent years because much of its congregation moved away, spreading farther from the city, and the Episcopal Diocese hesitated to put money into the church's upkeep. Finally recognizing its historical and architectural importance (the church, its rectory and its old graveyard are National Landmarks), the Diocese asked New York State for financial restoration aid. The state's Department of Parks, Division of Historic Preservation, put up money for an historic site survey and after that made a grant for reconstruction. The Diocese, the city of Mt. Vernon, and the Town of Eastchester bore the rest of the cost, and Eastchester's Department of Planning and Community Development coordinated the project.

Lightning had struck the church several times, perhaps an expression of heavenly disapproval or perhaps merely of recognition, heavily damaging the church tower. The tower was, in fact, according to architect James Corrado Piccone, who undertook plans for the reconstruction, in danger "of imminent collapse." Piccone put a steel, channel stabilizing frame into the tower, replaced damaged sandstone sections and repointed the masonry. And as a final precaution, he installed a lightning protection system.

Renovation

Old Port Exchange is a six-block waterfront district in downtown Portland, Maine. Since the late 1960s, the area's brick and granite commercial buildings have undergone a rejuvenation that has not only saved the area from demolition but has also turned it, in a few years, into the city's major tourist attraction. Its welter of new, small, ground-level retail shops compete successfully with suburban shopping malls, and the area's success has led the city to plan broadly, both within the Old Port Exchange and throughout Portland, for renovation and preservation.

Portland is one of the U.S.'s oldest Atlantic ports. Its waterfront buildings date from the late 18th to the early 20th centuries. Many have survived years of neglect with their original building components and embellishments intact. As the area languished, the economics of restoration became attractive to a few bold, private entrepreneurs. The story is a familiar one, for it is happening with increasing frequency.

As with most renewal projects today, this one was initiated by private individuals. It was not so much a project as a slow growth of restoration, one building's rebirth spurring another's, until real estate brokers, banks and other private sources, which had been initially hesitant, came in. Last to join was the city, which stepped in in 1972 with urban-renewal funds for brick sidewalks, street furniture, landscap-

**Old Port Exchange Area
Preservation**
Portland, Me.

Designers: Sasaki Assoc.,
and Moriece and Gary
(for City of Portland)

Clients: City of Portland:
Donald E. Megathlin, planning
director. Old Port Exchange
Association and other
Portland businesses,
organizations and citizens

ing and new lighting along Lower Exchange Street **(1)**. This first tentative city effort worked so well that help came from the National Endowment for the Arts. Using both a City Edges Grant and a City Options Grant, from NEA, Portland established an improvement program for its entire waterfront; moreover, these grants encouraged the city's attitude toward historic preservation and helped it launch a comprehensive historic preservation program for both waterfront and residential neighborhoods. Now, the city sees its program of public improvements as an essential complement to private restoration.

Currently underway in the Old Port Exchange are efforts

by a non-profit arts group to get a Cultural Facilities Grant with which to study the feasibility of turning the Milk Street Armory into a performing arts center. The city, in its newly determined role as helpmate, is applying to NEA for a Livable City Grant to implement suggestions made in its earlier Old Port Exchange planning. It wants three things:

1. To plan for public access to the waterfront.
2. To study the feasibility of reusing vacant upper-story space in Old Port Exchange.
3. To work out a detailed public improvements program for the area.

Mercantile Wharf Building
Boston, Mass.

Designers: John Sharratt Assoc., Inc., architects

Client: Mercantile Associates

Built on landfill in 1856, the Mercantile Wharf Building **(1)**, with its 18 bays for sail-makers and ships' chandlers, once stretched out into Boston Harbor. Today, it is a block or so from the Harbor **(2)**, fronting on Waterfront Park, backed up to the Fitzgerald Expressway. Landfill has spread beyond the building, leaving it landbound, and it is not incidental that its new uses relate to the land rather than to the harbor.

Renovated by architects John Sharratt Associates, Inc., the Mercantile Building is now a mixture of housing and retail shops. Shops ring the ground floor, opening both off the street and off a landscaped interior mall, cut through the interior of the building. This central atrium began to take shape as the ships' chandlers, who originally used the building, began to leave, and six of the original interior bays were pulled down to create uninterrupted interior space. Now, the apartments open on five levels off corridors overlooking the expanded central, skylit atrium. Skylights let light into upper-floor apartments **(6)**.

On the ground and top floors brick arches **(4)** span the corridors surrounding the atrium. And from the central space one can see remnants of the old brick bay bearing walls supporting the corridors **(3)**.

With its granite facade cleaned, the Mercantile Wharf Building is an outstanding backdrop for Waterfront Park. Little of the facade was changed, though new windows were put in and a pedestrian arcade entrance formed behind glass panels along Richmond Street and a café put there. Shops ring the building, their large glass windows overlooking the street through keystone arches **(5)**. Were it not for the freeway cutting overhead beyond the building's Cross Street entrance, Mercantile Wharf would relate to the Faneuil Hall Marketplace.

By having the site declared an urban renewal zone, the developers gained financial help from tax-exempt, interest-subsidized (section 266) state bonds, floated by the Massachusetts Housing Finance Authority.

**Kearns/Daynes
Building/Alley Annex**
Salt Lake City, Utah

Designers: Boyd A. Blackner
and Assoc., architect: William
D. Erickson, Craig L. Ames,
project team

Though its front facade sprouted a series of neon signs, and its ground-floor store-front was cut up and altered for a succession of shops, its old stones held their dignity and strength well enough for Salt Lake City's Daynes Building (named after a jeweler who once owned it) to be put on both the state and national Registers of Historic Buildings. But the building, built in 1890, was too small to justify an elevator or air-conditioning equipment, so its upper stories, in recent years, were vacant.

Next to the Daynes Building stands the Kearns Building, at 11 stories one of Salt Lake City's finest office towers, beautifully constructed (in the 1920s), well-maintained, and equipped to satisfy contemporary building codes.

The salvation of the Daynes Building was to plug it into its more substantial neighbor. By enclosing the alley between them **(2)** in glass and steel, and connecting the two buildings at each of their first four floors, they can share the larger structure's air conditioning, electricity and elevators. More than that, by moving the internal stairs of the smaller Daynes Building, piece by piece, out into the connecting

Client: Standard Buildings
Inc.: Doug Schilling, building
manager

structure **(1)**, which also has office space **(4)**, all the Daynes
Building's interior space is left for offices. Now that the building satisfies the current building code, its space rents for
rates comparable to those of surrounding offices.

Renovation included exposing, washing, sandblasting
and sealing the brick facades and refinishing and restoring
the building's heavy wood timbers and metal decoration.
The renovators had to stitch the wood framing together with
tension rods to meet earthquake restrictions, and install a
sprinkler system. At the rear of the Daynes Building is a
new, outside set of fire stairs **(3)**. The right of way, which still
runs at ground level, through the new addition, comes out
near these fire stairs and eventually there will be a small
park there, and brick walkways leading to other buildings on
the block.

The addition is a buffer between the two buildings, cutting
heat loss through their adjacent walls and serving as what
the architects call a "seismic hinge." A small central air-
conditioner in the Daynes Building carries the hot-spot air-
conditioning needs of the Kearns Building during summer.

Turtle Bay Towers
New York, N.Y.

Designers: Bernard Rothzeid
and Partners, architects

Client: Rockrose
Development Corporation

Rarely does a contemporary apartment building offer such a variety of apartment configurations. Achieved by solving what the architects describe as a "planning problem comparable to three-dimensional chess," the layouts in Turtle Bay Towers **(3)** manage to relate the plumbing of kitchens and baths, juggle the 20 different multiple setbacks (the result of earlier zoning incentives) and to provide bedrooms equal in number to half the apartments. This latter mandate is a regulation of New York City's J-51 legislation, which provides tax abatements to developers who convert commercial and industrial properties to residential use.

New York, of course, has seen a steady attrition of manufacturing lofts, as the cost of doing business in the city becomes increasingly unprofitable. Under J-51, though, if the city loses the manufacturing, it does not necessarily lose the building. To qualify for J-51, a building must have a certificate of occupancy from the city's Department of Buildings, which says that the building meets city standards for residential structures. The certificate is important, for with it a conversion can qualify for exemption from certain local real estate taxes, and an abatement or reduction in other local taxes. Besides, any increase in the assessed value of the building resulting from the conversion is exempted from all local taxes for 12 years. So a converter's taxes don't go up immediately, and he can get tax abatement of up to 8.33 percent of the conversion's cost, an abatement that may actually be more than the taxes. If so, he can carry over the abatement into the years after it normally would have expired.

The old building (1929) at 310 East 46th Street suffered a gas explosion in 1974, which ripped off one facade and destroyed the passenger elevator core. Fortunately these elevators had been near the edge of the building, and the renovators merely cleared the shaft space for an open court, converting the former service elevators to passenger elevators. In return for creating a court to bring in light and air, the building code allowed the renovators more apartment space elsewhere in the building; they took advantage of this provision by glassing in portions of the multiple setbacks under greenhouse-like canopies, extending the space in some apartment rooms **(2)**. Rooms are generally spacious, largely because of the building's 12 ft. ceiling height. But the architects maximize the space by putting lofts into most of the studio apartments and some of the one-bedroom units. These lofts can be used as sleeping or working spaces and have storage compartments in their bases. Besides, they break up, visually, what is often long, narrow apartment space **(1)**.

At street level, shops line both 45th and 46th Street and a step-down mirrored lobby leads to the elevator bank. Because the service elevator cabs are bigger than the current code allows passenger cabs to be, the renovators merely put in a glass-walled terrarium at the rear of each cab.

Exeter Street Theatre Building
Boston, Mass.

Designers: CBT/Childs Bertman Tseckares and Casendino, Inc., architects. T.G.I. Friday's, consultant architect: Melvin R. Fain

The Exeter Street Theatre Building, a Romanesque landmark in Boston's Back Bay, designed by William C. Richardson of Hartwell and Richardson in 1885 **(1)**, is still the Exeter Street Theatre, but it is now a lot more. Besides the movie theater, the building is now home to a restaurant, Exeter Street Friday's **(4)**, and to a third-floor suite of offices serviced by a separate entrance and a private elevator.

Originally built as the First Spiritualist Temple, the building had its interior rearranged in 1914 to include an art theater and third-floor living quarters for its trustees, the Berlin sisters. The sisters converted a 1,200-seat lecture hall on the second floor into the movie theater and for almost 60 years showed films, usually art films, to help support the temple's religious and philosophical work. But film attendance dwindled. By 1973 their film offerings were attracting so few patrons that they had to sell the building. It is a massive structure of brownstone and granite 94 ft. high, 90 ft. wide and 110 ft. long. And though developer Neil St. John Raymond vowed to preserve it, to do so he needed to find uses for it that would generate income.

His solution, worked out with the agreement and support of the Back Bay Neighborhood Association and the Back Bay Historical Commission, was to keep and refurbish the theater, add a restaurant with a glass canopy along the Newbury Street facade, and convert the third floor into 7,000 sq. ft. of office space for a single tenant.

All the changes were inspired. The theater's wooden seats were uncomfortable, so Raymond installed new, upholstered seats. The architects opened up the old lobby **(2)**, taking out the original oak-paneled walls and creating arched openings to the stairs and balcony. They had oak moldings made to match existing panels and brought in iron

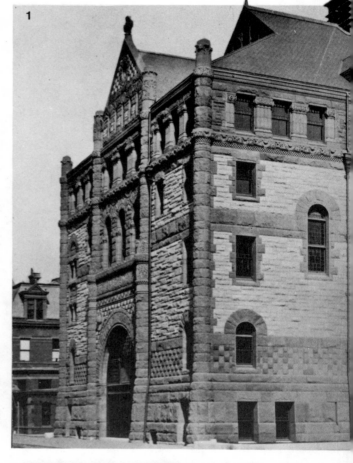

railings from other old buildings. The result is a look that fits the old temple and yet pays contemporary attention to light and open space **(3)**.

On the third floor is now 7,000 sq. ft. of executive office space for a single firm. To make this space attractive to a lessee, the architects put in a separate entrance on Newbury Street, installed a private elevator and a new electrical system. Upstairs, the space retains much of its original character; restored are its ceilings, leaded glass windows and oak paneling.

Easily the most noticeable change is the greenhouse-like aluminum and glass frame that runs for 80 ft. along the Newbury Street facade. Beneath it is part of Exeter Street Friday's restaurant, which occupies 8,150 sq. ft. of the building's basement and first-floor space. Hanging plants, Tiffany-style hanging lamps, and diners are visible from the street **(5)**; the greenhouse, though not of the period of the building, enhances its architecture, and just as importantly, eases the abruptness with which the building meets the street. Neighborhood residents had complained that the stark, fortress-like wall of the theater broke up the street's rhythm. Newbury Street is a shopping area. Its four- and five-story row houses have basement and first-floor shops and restaurants, and the Exeter Street Theatre's new restaurant engages the building in the street activity.

With the help of local neighborhood and historic commissions, the developer gained a zoning variation that allowed both office and retail use in the same building; by arguing that the building contained only three usable levels in its 94 ft. height, instead of a more usual size, the developer was able to reduce some of the building's supporting equipment.

Paramount Arts Centre
Aurora, Ill.

Designers: Elbasani Logan Severin Freeman, architect: Geoffrey Freeman, principal-in-charge; Peter Aaron, project designer. Frazier, Orr, Fairbank and Quam, construction supervision architects: Charles G. Pederson, project supervisor. Dean Abbott, landscape consultant.

Client: Aurora Redevelopment Commission and Aurora Civic Center Authority: Vernon L. Croxen, chairman; Gregory L. Gilmore, general manager; Deborah J. Kramp, project representative.

Rapp and Rapp were architects for Aurora, Illinois' Paramount movie theatre, which went up during the Depression for a million dollars. It had a pipe organ, a vaudeville stage and 1,885 seats; when it opened in 1931, its owner, J. J. Rubens, called it "Aurora's most precious jewel." He hired airplanes to drop rose petals on crowds which came out for its inaugural.

Forty-seven years later, the Paramount had a second opening, this time as a performing arts center. Transformed by Elbasani Logan Severin Freeman, of New York, with Frazier, Orr, Fairbank and Quam, of Aurora, from vaudeville house-movie theater to a house for legitimate theater, dance and symphony performances, the new Paramount opened in 1978. Its restoration took $2.95 million, and the new theater has the spirit of the old one, with its Art Deco-Art Nouveau interior and its two-story, light-bulb-encrusted Paramount sign above a marquee **(2)** built from the original plans.

Almost every restoration has heroes. This one had Conrad Schmidt. Schmidt offered to paint the elaborate lobby frieze patterns for free when the architects suggested leaving the lobby a solid color to cut costs. Schmidt's artisans "pounced" stencils of the Egyptianesque wall and ceiling patterns throughout the theater, then painted them in by hand.

Not all the restoration is exact. Inside, the main floor and balcony profiles were changed slightly to produce better sight lines **(4)**. But the original seating, cleaned, painted, resprung and reupholstered, is still there, and the mezzanine and its lobby are restored in the Art Deco-Art Nouveau style.

To make room for musical comedy and symphony orchestras, the architects extended an apron thrust stage ten ft. beyond the old proscenium and created a new proscenium that incorporates existing ornamental columns on either side of the stage. They also extended the stage to the rear, enlarging the flytower and putting in two additional floors of dressing rooms. To improve acoustics, they placed hard panels behind the sound absorbent murals at the sides **(1)** and rear of the house.

Outside, workmen cleaned and repaired the patterned brick and terra cotta insets. Along the Fox River (downtown Aurora is on an island) the badly deteriorated side wall was rebuilt and landscaped **(3)**, tying it in to other street work— part of Aurora's downtown redevelopment, which is being financed partly by racetrack earnings. The theater restoration is being paid for by State of Illinois bonds, bonds serviced by racetrack receipts.

To a large extent, the effect of the Paramount will depend on its relationship to the town. Its current uses will, of course, bring people into the area, but will the restored building spur other downtown renewal? The answer seems to be a qualified yes. Already planned for a site across Galena Boulevard is a complex of city offices, convention-exhibition space and shops and restaurants. A pedestrian bridge will connect the Performing Arts Center with the complex (see site plan).

**Corporate Offices for
Hershey Foods**
Hershey, Pa.

Designers: Wallace, McHarg, Roberts and Todd, architects: William Roberts, principal in charge; Charles Tomlinson, associate; William Becker, project architect; John Czarnowski, assistant architect

Client: Hershey Foods Corporation

When the founder of the Hershey Chocolate Company, Milton S. Hershey, died, his home was turned into a country club and surrounded by a golf course. The club added a one-story locker room extension just south of the house's rear wing in around 1940.

Originally constructed near the turn of the century (about 1905) by architect C. Emlen Urban of Lancaster, Pa., the house is stone **(1)** with a grand porch whose roof is supported by four ionic columns **(2)**. Four ionic pilasters, on the front facade, echo these columns. By renovating the house (and its locker room extension) for use as its corporate headquarters, Hershey Foods Corporation increased the house's historic visibility, gave its top executives an envi-

ronment protected from the bustle and distraction of the nearby factories, and saved the corporation some money by taking advantage of accelerated depreciation for renovation of certified historic structures.

Architects Wallace, McHarg, Roberts and Todd, of Philadelphia, who did the renovation, turned the locker room into office space for eight vice presidents and secretarial and administrative staff. Above these offices is a roof garden. The old house itself, with much of its wood, stained glass **(3)**, moldings and paneling restored, houses public spaces on its first floor, and offices for the corporation's three senior officers on its second.

The architects thought of the structure as having four

discrete functional zones with a net usable area of 20,000 sq. ft.:

Zone 1. The western portion of the ground floor, originally containing the living and dining rooms, library and game rooms, became a board room, conference room, lounges and executive dining room.

Zone 2. The eastern portion of the ground floor works with the former locker room as the principal office-clerical space (see floor plan). A ring of perimeter offices surround a skylighted secretarial space and within that is a core of conference room, library, storage and filing rooms.

Zone 3. The second-floor executive offices open onto the roof garden.

Zone 4. Exercise and locker rooms, the vault, storage and duplication rooms and the building's mechanical space are in the basement.

The corporate gesture of restoring the old mansion gives the community a source of continuity and pride.

Renovation was done under Section 2124 of Public Law 94-455 of the 1976 Tax Reform Act. This law allows accelerated depreciation over five years for historically certified structures whose improvements are also certified by the Department of the Interior. The Hershey mansion's renovation is one of the first projects in Pennsylvania to take advantage of the new law.

ABC Armory/Studio and 66th/67th Street Redevelopment
New York, N.Y.

Designers: Kohn Pedersen Fox Associates PC, architects, planners and interior designers: A. Eugene Kohn, partner-in-charge; Sheldon Fox, partner-in-charge; William Pedersen, design partner; Patricia Conway, planning partner; Paul Rosen, project designer; Michael Gordon, project coordinator;

Robert Cioppa, project manager-Armory; John Harris, project manager-WABC/TV; Richard Sowinski, project manager-30 West 67th Street

Client: American Broadcasting Companies, Inc.

Though dissimilar in appearance, these two armories may be typical of American attitudes in the 1970s. Converted from their previous military uses to peaceful ones, and both having to do, in different ways, with the arts, they were attractive to the converters because of their sound structures, high ceilings and large, open interior spaces.

ABC Armory Studio

ABC could have built a new studio space somewhere on West 66th or 67th Streets. In fact, when the company purchased the old Armory at 56 West 66th Street from New York City, which was using it as a public tennis court, ABC executives considered pulling it down. But their need for new studio space was so urgent, and the hazards of demolishing a neighborhood landmark so apparent, that the company decided to use the Armory's 13,000 sq. ft., three-story, clear-span drill hall as a TV production studio and to convert the remaining 31,600 sq. ft. to space for supporting facilities. Helping them decide was the city's law No. 976, providing tax abatement for some renovation and reuse projects.

ABC's decision means that this mostly residential neighborhood, only a block or so from Lincoln Center, will retain a local landmark. Steam-cleaned, the Armory's facade turned out to be a cheerful one of polychrome brick and limestone **(1,2)**, and though the structure is not overwhelmingly handsome and its new use not precisely suited to its previous interior space, the neighborhood gains stability and spirit from the restoration.

Inside, ABC uses the old drill hall as a 10,000 sq. ft. studio. In the rebuilt basement are 17,500 sq. ft. of dressing, makeup, wardrobe, locker and storage rooms and mechanical space. On the first floor, in partitioned space around the studio, are 7,500 sq. ft. of control, lighting and prop rooms, a reception area and a loading dock. Right above all this is a second floor of space partitioned for production offices, and above that is 4,300 sq. ft. of mechanical space. ABC is also building on vacant lots in the neighborhood. Already, two buildings are completed, one of which supports the armory studio. Keeping these building profiles low, ABC claims it will reestablish the original 67th Street roofline.

Cultural Arts Center
Columbus, Ohio

Designers: Schooley Cornelius Assoc., architects

Client: City of Columbus, Department of Recreation and Parks

Columbus Arsenal Cultural Arts Center

Built in 1860 with convict labor for "not in excess of $14,000," the Columbus Armory by the early 1970s found itself stranded, surrounded by parking lots. Across the street, though, was a new riverfront park. And when the city leased the abandoned armory from the state in 1976, city agencies saw the preservation of the Armory as the provision of an anchor, preventing further deterioration of the southwest Columbus riverfront area, and as a commitment by the city to its own redevelopment.

On architectural grounds alone, the Armory's preservation is commendable. Its particular variation of Italianate architecture, its brick, cast-iron and timber construction are found in few remaining buildings of any significance (1). Since 1974, the Armory has been on the National Register of Historic Places.

Columbus's decision was to open the building to as many people and programs as possible; to this end, though it is essentially the new home of the city's expanded arts and crafts program (under the Department of Recreation and Parks), it holds other activities in its outside courtyard and its exhibit and meeting spaces, making it an extension of the park across the street.

The Armory's large, open interior spaces lent themselves to those of a Cultural Arts Center. Architects Schooley Cornelius Associates located activities within the building according to how much noise they generate and how well they go together. On the main floor are a museum, spaces for exhibits and theatrical performances (or meetings) and for offices. By using low partitions throughout, the architects tried to maintain the building's open interior.

A shed adjoining one side of the main building holds shops for woodworking, sculpture, jewelry, enameling, ceramics and pottery, and at one end of the shed, beyond the main building, are a sandcasting pit and kiln.

The second floor's central space is a weaving studio with looms and a silk-screening area (3). On a mezzanine overlooking part of the weaving studio is space for graphic arts, photography and framing. The building's towers hold staircases and offices (2). The building was cleaned and sealed; new windows and doors were put in and the garden wall rebuilt around a concrete block core, using the original bricks.

Work progressed in stages, financed initially by a bond issue, revenue-sharing funds and money from the Parks Department improvement fund. A second and final phase drew money from an Economic Development Administration grant.

Total cost of the renovation to date: less than $2 million. The city has a 99-year lease at $1 per year.

Lutheran Medical Center
Brooklyn, N.Y.

Designers: Rogers, Butler, Burgun and Shahine, architects: J. Armand Burgun, partner-in-charge; William F. Adkinson, project architect; Michelle J. Zoller, Stephanie Mallis, project designers; Jamie Hanson, supergraphics and signage. Balsley, Balsley, Kuhl, landscape architects. Turner Construction Co., contractors

In what may have been the first transformation of its kind, the abandoned American Machine and Foundry Company plant in southwest Brooklyn became the Lutheran Medical Center—bright, clean, efficient. The recycling helped the community symbolically, by presenting it with a monumental example of halted blight. And, of course, it helps physically by giving the lower- and middle-income persons who live nearby access to a major hospital.

But the medical center itself benefited from the transformation. The old factory offered a sound, sturdy, five-story shell, with 600,000 sq. ft. of floor space, all of it capable of supporting 250 pounds per sq. ft. Floor to floor height was 16 ft. 7 in., enough to allow easy installation of lighting and communications equipment and the welter of air-conditioning, heating and electrical ducts. Besides being cleaned, given new glazing (mirror-glazed, blocked on the

Client: Lutheran Medical
Center: George Adams,
president

inside to reduce heat loss — except in patient rooms, where windows open) and painted hospital-white, the structure was left much as it had been. Only a new front entrance and elevator/escalator core, with eight elevators and two escalators, changes the exterior configuration **(2,4)**.

To gut the old factory, the contractor took bulldozers inside, clearing space for new boilers, emergency power systems, radiant heat and for air conditioning and heat recovery wheels.

On the new hospital's top three floors are six medical and surgical units, with ten major operating rooms, two cystologic operation rooms, four delivery rooms, two special procedure operating rooms, an ambulatory care unit and ten radio graphic and fluoroscopic rooms.

Eighty percent of patient rooms are double rooms **(3)**. Entrance is through an extensive second floor lobby **(1)**.

DECK LINKED
ION. USE FOR
TIVE LECTURES

BARRIER PLANTING
SLOPE. PRARIE RO
HAWTHORNE THICKE

Natural Environment

Enhancement of Urban Open Space

Conservation of the Natural Landscape

Emil T. Micha

Enhancement
of Urban Open Space

On the floor of Citicorp Center's seven-story atrium, surrounded by trees, is a 250-seat café **(1)**. On a fold-out stage, at one edge of the café, musicians, mimes, jugglers and comics often entertain. This space is the focus of the Market at Citicorp, a complex of 20 shops and restaurants that have replaced and refocused the street level neighborhood retail activity displaced by Citicorp Center, the complex of church, retail building, and 59-story office tower that rises above and around the Market on what was a low-rise mid-Manhattan block. Taking up three levels of the seven-story atrium-galleria (see section), the Market provides the odors of perking coffee, of rare tobaccos, exotic pastry and bouquets of freshly-cut flowers, the sounds of music, of forks hitting chinaware and of people talking. There is activity and color from dawn to midnight. And that is the way Citibank and its designers planned it.

The subway stop at 53rd Street and Lexington Avenue empties into the plaza just outside the Market (see plan) and this plaza, with its broad stairs descending through a water sculpture, is meant both as a place of repose and a lure to channel people into the Market. The designers widened the Lexington Avenue sidewalk from 13 to almost 24 ft. so that they could tuck retail shops beneath the sidewalk fronting on the sunken plaza. And a special zoning resolution let them sink the plaza 17 ft. beneath grade instead of a standard maximum of three ft. They also needed a zoning resolution to allow the office tower, which stands on gigantic stilts 112 ft. above the plaza, to stretch out over the plaza, obstructing the sky.

The mixture of uses works, keeping the Market filled with color, motion and people long after offices close at 5 p.m. Shopping and scheduled performances lure people to the area on weekends. Shops and restaurants in the Market reflect Citibank's world-wide activities. Restaurants are Italian, Swiss, Greek, French, Hungarian, Scandinavian, English and American, and shops carry international goods.

Designers: Halcyon, Ltd., retail development. Hugh Stubbins and Assoc., architects. Emery Roth and Sons, associated architects. Sasaki Assoc., landscape architects and plaza developers. D.I. Design and Development, design consultants. Designetics Assoc., Inc., lighting

Client: Citicorp: Henry deFord III, senior vice president; Gerard P. Beitel, assistant vice president

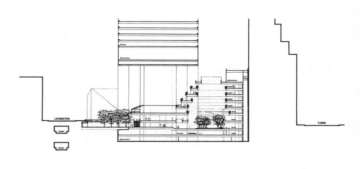

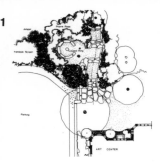

Lighthouse Landing Park
Evanston, Ill.

Designers: Johnson, Johnson and Roy Inc., planners and landscape architects; Metz, Train, Olson and Youngren, Inc., architects

Client: Evanston Department of Parks, Recreation and Forestry

Lighthouse Landing Park is 10.4 acres on the shore of Lake Michigan in Evanston, Ill., a few blocks north of the Northwestern University campus. Welded together from three parcels of land, one formerly owned by the Deering family of International Harvester Corp., one by utilities magnate Harley Clarke, and one by the Grosse Point Lighthouse, the park suffered from neglect inherent in disparate management by five distinct groups.

Park uses include:

1. A swimming beach, administered by the city's Recreation Board.
2. An area of grass, trees, and playground equipment administered by the Evanston Environmental Association as a teaching organic garden.
3. An open meadow of 2.4 acres with a small picnic shelter, administered by the city's Northeast Park District.
4. The former Harley Clarke estate. The main house is administered by the Evanston Art Center as a gallery and workshop. The estate's coach house is rented to private tenants. A green house, attached to the old coach house, is used by the Environmental Association for teaching.
5. The southernmost section of the park, containing the lighthouse, is administered by the Lighthouse Park District, which provides space in the lighthouse's outbuildings for a Nature Center Museum administered by the Evanston Environmental Association.

With landscaping by the noted Swedish landscape architect Jens Jensen, the Clarke property had once been a showplace. The house, designed by Richard Powers to resemble a 16th-century English Tudor mansion, was given a 1927 award as "Best Residence" by the Evanston Art Commission **(5)**. Part of the plan, worked out recently for the city by architects Metz, Train, Olson and Youngren, Inc. and landscape architects Johnson, Johnson and Roy, is to restore and retain as much of the house and grounds **(4, 5)** as possible. The plan would also have the adjoining 19th-century lighthouse **(1, 4)** restored and maintained as a museum.

But the crux of the plan is to bring some organization to the park. With four sections of the park administered by five separate agencies and private groups, it needs some sort of overall administration as badly as it needs restoration and maintenance. Called for by the plan is a joint commission to administer an Activities Management Plan, a management program worked out initially by attorneys of the five agencies and agreed to by all. Sitting on the commission would be representatives of the agencies.

While recognizing the need for central control, the planners saw no need to change current park uses. After meetings with community leaders and individuals, the planners suggested strongly that the park's physical arrangement and use be continued without adding major amenities, such as more parking space. In fact, if followed, the plan will strictly control parking on park roads and seek additional parking space from Northwestern University or nearby lots.

In all, three plans emerged. The second is a land-use and site improvement plan, and the third a restoration plan. The plans are detailed and, if followed, can no doubt be effective. But the crux of the matter is the Management Plan. If the parties involved cannot cooperate within the scope of their activities and budgets, nothing will happen. But if the steps and time goals suggested by the planners are met, Lighthouse Landing Park can become a place even more attractive to swimmers, picnickers, nature lovers, artists, children and history buffs than it already is.

4

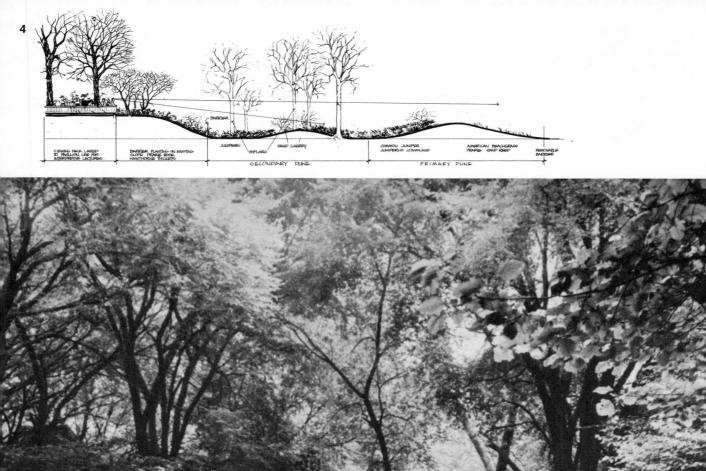

VIEWING DECK LINKED TO PAVILLON, USE FOR INTERPRETIVE LECTURES.

BARRIER PLANTING ON EXISTING SLOPE. PRAIRIE ROSE. HAWTHORNE THICKETS.

JUNIPERS

POPLARS   SAND CHERRY

COMMON JUNIPER
JUNIPERUS COMMUNIS

AMERICAN BEACHGRASS
PRAIRIE SAND REED

REMOVABLE BARRIER

SECONDARY DUNE   PRIMARY DUNE

**Mill Hill Historic
Park/Douglass Place**
Trenton, N.J.

Designers: Trenton
Department of Planning and
Development: John P. Clarke,
Fred Travisano, architects;
Philip B. Caton, James
Greenberg, Lee Weintraub,
project design team.
Schnadelback Braun
Partnership, landscape
architects

Client: City of Trenton

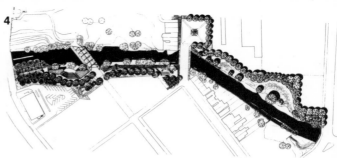

In 1905, Olmsted Associates suggested that Trenton, N.J., use the land along Assunpink Creek for a linear park. Olmsted envisioned romantic plantings along the water that would lend an inviting, lazy aura to the creek as it wound through downtown Trenton. The city was not ready for an Assunpink Park then, and in subsequent years the creek suffered the fate of most urban waterways: it became a receptacle for pollution. But, of course, the mood eventually changed in Trenton, and though the park, designed and recently constructed along Assunpink Creek by the city's Department of Planning and Development, may not be romantic, at least its conception pays homage to Olmsted's suggestion. A planning department rendering of what the park might become shows a musician in tails playing a grand piano in a small quayside amphitheater while small boys sit fishing nearby and couples stroll along the water beneath lacy-leafed trees (3). The actuality (2) is not too much different.

First step in creation of Mill Hill Historic Park was to control what neighboring communities could dump into the creek. As the creek's water quality improved, so did attitudes toward the creek and the proposed adjoining park.

Situated in Trenton's Mercer-Jackson Neighborhood Renewal Area, the park stretches for 1,000 ft. along Assunpink Creek (4), covering, in all, six acres. These acres are planned to include what the neighborhood residents wanted in a park. Indeed, the planning was done by an interdisciplinary team that included not only professional architects and planners from the Trenton Department of Planning and Development and private consultant landscape architects, but also a committee of neighborhood residents, the Project Advisory Committee. This team set objectives for the park and explored alternative ways to meeting them, then took these alternatives to the neighborhood in workshops. Thus the entire neighborhood stayed close to the design and planning as they progressed. Almost everyone wanted a plan that would do more than just contain the creek, something that would make the creek a part of overall neighborhood redevelopment.

The site is historic. It was here that Washington and his troops fought the Second Battle of Trenton, defeating Cornwallis on January 2, 1777. Earlier still, in the 1670s, the creekbanks held Trenton's earliest industry, a grist mill which led to the growth nearby of Mill Hill, the city's first residential area.

Parts of the still-standing mill wall are preserved in the park, which has fieldstone terraces stepping down to the water and a waterside promenade. A statue of George Washington commemorates the battle (1). To make sure that ground water could percolate through all this construction to the creek, the city used gabions, rock-filled wire baskets, which, when set together, act as dry walls, holding back the banks while allowing the normal flow of groundwater. Also in the park is a small amphitheater and Douglass Place, with the statue of Washington, where concerts, fairs, bazaars and exhibitions can take place. There are playthings for children, and perhaps most importantly, there are places where people can walk or sit to enjoy the trees and water in the midst of a bustling city.

Lots of sand, trees, water and colorful canvas squares set the tone for a demonstration playground project that will let handicapped and able-bodied children play together, sharing the same experiences with the same equipment. Landscape architect Hisham N. Ashkouri designed the playground as an entry in a competition sponsored by the New York City Planning Department and the Department of Parks and Recreation and Cultural Affairs, and though its components are not strikingly different from those in other playgrounds, Ashkouri has modified traditional things such as swings and slides to make them workable for less agile children. Swings, for instance, can be operated by hand. A

child can hoist himself into the harness-like swing from a wheelchair and put the swing in motion by pulling on a chain instead of pushing with his feet. Slides have two chutes, side by side, one conventional, the other a stepped incline up which a child can hoist himself backwards using his arms. At the top, he merely sidles over to the conventional chute, and slides down to his wheelchair.

But Ashkouri also added attractions found in few, if any, other playgrounds. There is an 1880s railroad with flatcars equipped with the same kind of pump-like propulsion device that old-fashioned hand cars had; children work the pump with their hands and arms to make the cars go. A traffic

Designer: Hisham N. Ashkouri, architect and urban designer

Client: Department of Parks and Recreation, New York City. Department of New York City Planning Special Projects Unit: Saul Nimowitz, unit director and project director; David Mayerfeld, architectural coordinator; Mona Levine, project planner

game encourages children to propel their wheelchairs or tricycles through a pattern of road signs and signals. There is a rope-climbing net over a bed of sand. A water wheel, worked by children, moves water down a stream where other children can wade or wheel wheelchairs on warm summer days. Ashkouri thought about summer and sun in his design and as a result divided the playground's layout into three parts: a shaded playground area, a non-shaded playground and an open field for sports with trees and a picnic area nearby.

The park is being put together on 2.6 acres in Flushing Meadows-Corona Park in New York City and will go up with the aid of about $800,000 in Community Development funds.

To insure that the equipment is safe and vandal-proof, the construction contract is being bolstered by a separate testing contract, which may, of course, lead to modifications in the design.

The playground when completed will accommodate 150 children at once. By the time the park opens in the summer of 1979, it should be overbooked by New York City's 60,000 handicapped kids. They have other playgrounds, designed especially for them, but none where they can play along with their non-handicapped peers.

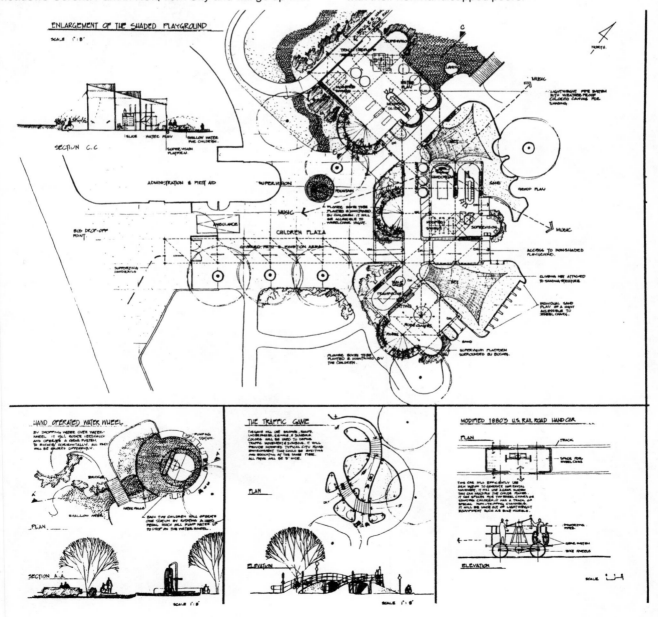

Josiah Quincy Community School, open space elements Boston, Mass.

Designers: The Architects Collaborative, Inc., architects: H. Morse Payne, David G. Sheffield, principals-in-charge; Martin Sokoloff, project architect. Quincy School Project: Hermann H. Field, concept planning and project development

Client: City of Boston Department of Public Facilities

Boston's South Cove is home to a mix of blacks, whites, Chinese and Puerto Ricans. Many speak no English and as a result have little sense of community beyond their own family and friends. Children from these homes, though they may be bright and outgoing, too often lag behind their peers in school. So the need to build a new Josiah Quincy Community School in South Cove was thought of as a chance to consolidate a fragmented, diffuse community. Initial impetus came from a pressing need for a new school building. The old one, the oldest elementary school structure in Boston, went up in 1847 and needed replacement. At the same time, the Tufts-New England Medical Center was planning to reach out into Boston, offering medical services through clinics to neighborhoods that lacked them. Why not combine school and medical center, went the thinking, and why not go beyond that, making the new building a focus of service for the entire South Cove area, a complex of community services.

Actually, the program went even further in a difficult but practical welding of service, housing and community recreation space. A housing tower, designed by Jung Brannen Associates, rises in air rights above one corner of the complex. This use of school air rights, which has been tried successfully elsewhere in the U.S., needed an amendment to the state condominium law; local zoning had to be changed to permit recreation space on the complex's rooftops instead of at grade. The entire project was difficult because of the complexity of its needs and the numbers of agencies, institutions, corporations and individuals involved. It took ten years of planning and large infusions of federal, state and private foundation funding, research and planning to complete the final complex.

Housed in the complex are the new Josiah Quincy School, capable of handling 800 students in four sub-schools, grouped around a library, which they all share, with mutual access to a swimming pool, gymnasium, cafeteria, auditorium and the roof-level recreation spaces. Also in the complex are a neighborhood health center, staffed by Tufts-New England personnel, offices for the Quincy School Community Council, the neighborhood's new-found collective voice, and for a little city hall. Visually and physically the community is given a focus and the complex tied to the community by the series of recreational terraces which step up from the street **(1)**. The Architects Collaborative (TAC), which several years ago designed the Tufts-New England Medical Center, designed the Quincy Community School so that these roof levels have considerable visual distinction. Ramps, stairs, walls all bring a variety of surfaces, angles and textures to the area, and these are augmented by those of play equipment and seating **(2)**. The spaces are truly urban in that they are formed of man-made materials, such as concrete and steel, rather than natural ones such as wood and earth.

The community can use the rooftop spaces and sometimes the swimming pool, gym, auditorium and library as well, when the school is not in session. The complex has become, with its porcelain panels of children's artwork running in thin bands along the school's roofline **(3)**, a beacon, bringing the community together, and more than that, though the open spaces lack greenery, a sort of village square, a focal point for a neighborhood that needs one. The Quincy Community School is a reminder to South Cove that it is a neighborhood, not just a haphazard collection of people with different ethnic backgrounds.

The Whittier Urban Design Framework
Minneapolis, Minn.

Designers: Team 70 Architects, Inc., urban design and planning: Bernard Jacob, principal-in-charge; John McNamara, project director; Richard Strong, assoc. project director; David Eijadi, Craig Anderson, Ronald Korsh, Sandra Becker, Joanne Kieffer, Clara Jacob, Gail Werren, project team. Assistance from the State of Minnesota Crime Control Planning Board.

Since 1940, the number of dwelling units in Whittier, an 83-block area of Minneapolis, has doubled. Though this area represents one percent of the city's land, 2.6 percent of the city's population now lives there, mostly in apartment houses built since World War II. At the turn of the century, Whittier was an area where Minneapolis's well-to-do had their homes. But taxes and population pressure changed all that. Now, most residents have average incomes and most of them are dissatisfied with the area. Sixty-one percent think it's not a good place to raise children.

Probably, the decay of Whittier would have continued were it not for the Dayton Hudson Foundation. Dayton's is one of Minneapolis's major retailers, and its most profitable store is its downtown one, not far from Whittier. So Dayton's has a stake in the future of Whittier, a stake enforced by its foundation's contributions to two Whittier-located institutions, the Children's Theater and the Minneapolis Society of Fine Arts. Recently, it increased that stake by foundation contributions of $300,000 for research into Whittier's problems and for implementation of the findings.

Obviously, the project was extensive, and to guide it a planning committee was formed, drawing representatives from existing neighborhood organizations, institutions, businesses and including some of the area's elected officials. Committee members started with careful inventories of the neighborhood's physical assets, its buildings and open spaces, its street and traffic circulation. They determined, for instance, just what each parcel of land in Whittier was being used for and the condition of each building, what the noise levels were at particular points and where crimes were taking place. More than that, they went into the community equipped with extensive questionnaires **(2)** asking residents (five percent of them) and businesses (50 percent) about open space, crime, housing, security and other reasons why they liked or disliked Whittier. Armed with the resulting statistics, the long-range planning committee held a series of public meetings in the area. More than 600 persons showed up at these meetings to identify community problems and discuss and approve ways of solving them. Through the entire process, the community was fortunate in having an existing communications device, a neighborhood newspaper, the *Whittier Globe*, to announce these meet-

1 Year 1 Action Plan

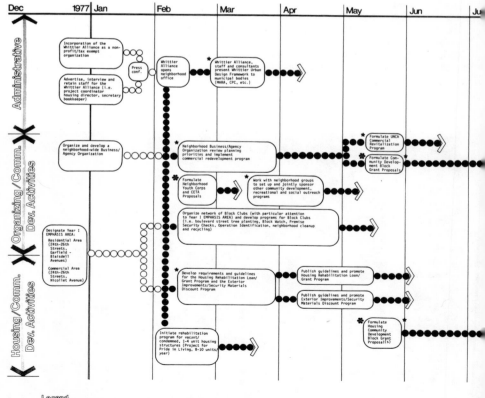

Client: Dayton Hudson Foundation, Minneapolis Society of Fine Arts, Minneapolis Star and Tribune Co., Northern States Power Co., Northwestern National Bank of Minneapolis, Northwestern Bell, Upper Loop Improvement Assoc.

ings and spread word of what happened at them.

Most of the detailed planning for what became the Whittier Urban Design Framework was handled by Team 70 Architects, Inc. **(1)**. Four major plans evolved to deal with (a) housing; (b) commercial redevelopment; (c) open space and pedestrian circulation; and (d) parking and vehicle circulation.

Inherent in these plans, the planners hope, are the solutions to the neighborhood's eight most pressing problems: building deterioration, lack of public services and public space maintenance, lack of neighborhood-oriented businesses and off-street parking, lack of private recreation space and private off-street parking, crime, lack of communications, and a lack of organized goals.

These changes are, according to Bernard Jacob of Team 70 Architects, "destined to bring about a positive change in the neighborhood's identity and image...The lack of identity, organized goals and power are, in large part, at the root of many of the neighborhood's problems."

To implement the plans, two changes have already taken place in Whittier. Newly organized block clubs help solve individual problems. These clubs plant trees, clean streets, and serve as a group voice with which to call for security. The second change is the formation of the Whittier Alliance, a non-profit community development corporation set up to implement neighborhood-wide programs. Because it is non-profit, the Alliance can funnel public and private money without administrative charges.

From the beginning, says a spokesman for the Dayton Hudson Foundation, "the Foundation knew that a project of this size and duration could not be accomplished with its resources alone. Therefore, from the very beginning, the project was viewed as a joint project of neighborhood residents, community groups, foundations, corporations and all levels of government. But no government money went into the initial planning. Helping the Dayton Hudson Foundation finance the first steps were the Minneapolis Society of Fine Arts, the *Minneapolis Star and Tribune*, Northern States Power Co., Northwestern National Bank of Minneapolis, Northwestern Bell and the Upper Loop Improvement Association.

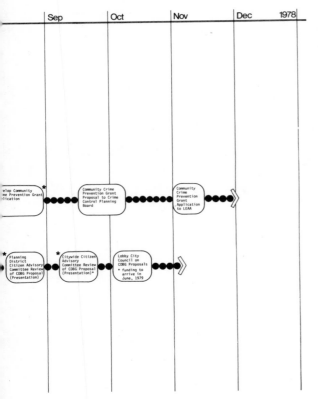

University of New Mexico Campus Tactual Map

Albuquerque, N.M.

Designers: Design and Planning Assistance Center: Howard Lee Greenstein, project director; Jim Graf, Howard Lee Greenstein, Brian Kuckleman, Matteo Moore, Rand Wilson, graphics and design team

Clients: Department of Special Services, University of New Mexico and Ad Hoc Committee of Visually Handicapped on Campus

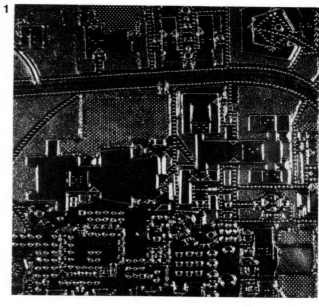

Tactual mapping is a relatively new concept. But prodded by sightless and visually impaired students and faculty at the University of New Mexico, Albuquerque's Design and Planning Assistance Center developed a lightweight booklet of eight detailed tactual maps that can guide students past campus hazards, such as bike racks, kiosks, planters, benches and steps, to the buildings or open public spaces they seek.

The university's Special Services Department underwrote the project, convinced that it was called for by Section 504 of the Federal Rehabilitation Act of 1973. The act, among other things, provides federal funds for a recipient to "ensure that no handicapped student is denied the benefits of, excluded from participation in, or otherwise subjected to discrimination under the education program or activity operated by the recipient because of the absence of educational auxiliary aids..."

The Design and Planning Assistance Center, a non-profit design organization, found little precedent for a tactual map. So, essentially, they designed their own with the aid of an ad hoc committee of sightless students. What emerged is a spiral-bound booklet, 12 in. by 11 in. and about one inch thick (3). Light enough to be carried easily, it consists of relief representations of campus areas (1). These reliefs are vacuum-formed in clear plastic sheets, which fit over maps printed with large type. These latter, more conventional maps are for use by students with low vision. Opposite the maps, on the facing pages, are braille keys (2) and explanations.

Guided by the students, the Design and Planning Assistance Center worked out the symbols and textures of what amounts to a tactual map language. Represented tactually are such physical campus features as water, parking, lawn, building entrance sidewalks, ramps and walls or fences.

The Center expects that not only will its maps help sightless students at the UNM become more independent but that the maps can also become a prototype for tactual maps of similar communities or institutions.

AREAL SYMBOLS		POINT SYMBOLS	
PLAZA OR LARGE PAVED AREA INDICATED BY BASE OF MAP			BUILDING IDENTIFICATION
	BUILDING		STEPS-OPEN SIDE IS BOTTOM OF FLIGHT
	BUILDING WITH TWO ENTRANCES		WIDE STEPS
	LAWN, DIRT, OR UNPAVED AREA		FOUR FLIGHTS OF STEPS
	PARKING	■	OBSTACLE
	WATER	•	TREE IN PAVED AREA
	ATHLETIC COURTS	° ○	PLANTERS, SEVERAL SIZES
LINE SYMBOLS		●	ORNAMENTAL WATER FOUNTAIN
....	SIDEWALK OR WALKWAY	∧	BENCH OR BENCH COMPLEX
‖‖ RAMP,	WIDE SIDE IS TOP	▶	CURB CUT
═══	STREET OR DRIVE	◖	BUS STOP
───	WALL OR FENCE		

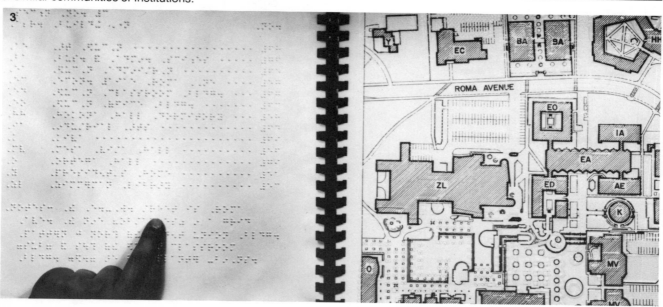

New York Self-Help Handbook: A Step-by-Step Guide to Neighborhood Improvement Projects
New York, N.Y.

Designers: Karin Carlson, text and research. Roger Whitehouse, graphic design, planning and production

Client: The Citizens Committee for New York City, Inc.

It's easy to make your neighborhood better looking and more enjoyable if you know how. Where do you start? New York City residents now have a handsome, easy-to-follow-and-understand guide to 106 projects that will brighten and strengthen their neighborhoods. Called the *New York Self Help Handbook,* it offers sensible, step-by-step information on how to adopt and care for a tree, how to organize a block association or a tenant patrol, how to start a weed-control project or one to stem erosion, how to form a purchasing club, and on and on. Each section offers step-by-step information about how to proceed, where to go for technical assistance (usually a city or private agency) and a brief

listing of what similar organizations in other parts of the city have done.

Written and researched by Karin Carlson, with graphics and production by Roger Whitehouse, the book was produced for the Citizens Committee for New York City with a grant from Manufacturers Hanover Trust. The Citizens Committee is a non-profit organization formed to catalyze private citizens and institutions into tackling the problems flowing from New York City's fiscal dilemma.

Though written specifically for New York, there is no reason the handbook can't be used beneficially by communities anywhere throughout the country.

Urban Open Space/Plaza Zoning
New York, N.Y.

Designers: Urban Design Group, New York Department of City Planning: Raquel Ramati, director, Michael Parley, deputy director. Julie Sahni, project director, Residential Plazas. Michael Parley, project director, Urban Open Space. Design team: Patrick Ping-Tze Too, Martin Dorf, Kuo Ming Tsu, Merry Neisner, Renee Kemp, Clifford Rodriguez, Dora Zhivotinsky, Kanubhai Vyas, Brunilda Mesa. Counsel's office: Norman Marcus, Fred Zauderer, Pares Bhattacharji. Consultants: William H. Whyte, Lauren Otis, Millard Humstone.

Client: New York City Planning Commission

Allowing developers a 20 percent floor-space bonus if they provided a plaza in proportion to the size of the building worked for New York City only in theory. The 1961 zoning ordinance did create some 20 acres of open space throughout the city in 15 years, but it fell far short of providing the quality of air, light and ambience that its designers intended. Too often the resulting plazas

- received no sunlight;
- were sunken below grade and inaccessible;
- were fenced off and closed to the public;
- had no place to sit;
- contained no plants or trees;
- were elevated above eye level, creating blank walls along sidewalks.

Some resulting plazas were, of course, true urban oases, inviting repose and spreading calm. But the letter of the zoning allowed such disregard for the city and its occupants that the New York City Planning Department's Urban Design Group felt the need to work out guidelines detailing exactly what these plazas should accomplish and how they should accomplish it. Walking a narrow line between the twin disasters of sterility from loopholes and sterility from over-legislation, the Urban Design Group came up with zoning regulations that they hope will make plazas extensions of New York street life, accessible to everyone, while still giving designers great latitude in execution.

These regulations, worked out after what is probably the most thorough study ever of plazas by a public agency, come in two versions, one for commercial properties, enacted in May 1975, and one for residential structures, enacted in April 1977.

Both sets of zoning regulations define standards meant to insure:

- adequate pedestrian circulation;
- maximum sunlight;
- seating;
- tree planting;
- accessibility by the handicapped;
- retail frontage along street and plaza;
- open air cafés, kiosks and other amenities;
- lighting;
- maintenance;
- proper plaza proportions and dimensions.

For instance, the regulations mandate that plazas be elevated no more than three feet above street-level nor more than three feet below it, so they can relate properly to the street. Gone will be the isolated, inaccessible sunken plaza (1) and the plaza raised so far above the street that a passing pedestrian sees only a blank wall.

For plazas at the base of a residential building (2), the regulations specify decorative paving. In addition, there must be lighting at a level of "not less than two horizontal foot candles during hours of darkness." Also set in some detail are seating (one linear foot of seating for each 30 sq. ft. of primary open space), tree planting (one tree per 1,000 sq. ft. of primary open space, and to insure that trees have a chance to survive, new plaza-trees must be at least three and a half to four inches in diameter, planted in at least 100 cubic ft. of soil, each with soil depth not less than three ft. six in.), bicycle parking facilities (two bike racks per 1,000 sq. ft. of primary open space), drinking fountains (one per plaza), and suggested, to nudge developers into thinking of the community, are such amenities as play equipment, game tables, sculpture, trellises and arbors, awnings, canopies, fountains and pools. But, lest a zealous builder cram his public space with amenities until there is no space, the zoning regulations read that all amenities "mandatory, additional and optional shall not exceed 60 percent of the primary space…" Cafés and shops are also suggested as amenities fronting on a plaza, and so that owners stand up to the responsibility of making these plazas public, the new zoning requires a plaque "at a prominent location within the plaza, visible from the sidewalk" saying plainly that the plaza is open to the public, and giving the name of the owner and the name and address of whomever maintains the space.

It is not surprising that author and social commentator William H. Whyte played a significant role in the Urban Design Group's decisions about the new zoning. For more than a decade, Whyte has dedicated himself to the study of urban open spaces and their use. His films, writing and knowledge guided the Urban Design Group as they measured and studied plazas to learn to judge proper proportion and features. The Urban Design Group also interviewed plaza users, some 500 of them, asking what they wanted from a plaza and why they used them. The Group also went to community organizations, asking them to review the zoning legislation as it was being written, and to professional groups such as the New York Chapter of the AIA, the Regional Plan Association, the Municipal Art Society and the American Society of Landscape Architects. Finally, for an analysis of plaza costs and leasing benefits, the Group went to real estate experts and builders.

The result, the City Planning Commission is betting, will be plazas that are not just barren, windswept concrete pads. Instead they will be extensions of the street, adding to the life of the city, open, sunlit, green with plantings, and, most of all, used by the city's people.

Conservation of the Natural Landscape

Suffolk County Farmland Preservation Program
Long Island, N.Y.

Designer: Office of Suffolk County Executive John V.N. Klein

Client: Suffolk County

Suffolk County, consisting of the eastern portion of Long Island, leads New York State in agricultural output. A recent estimate of the county's yearly agricultural sales stood at $70 million. But ironically, the county is burdened with a heavy, sometimes dense population that is growing rapidly as people push east from New York City 100 miles to the west (1). With 1.3 million residents, Suffolk is the state's second largest county, and it is not surprising that most of this population (92 percent) is packed into the towns closest to New York City. As Suffolk's population pushes east, it is following a pattern established nationwide, a pattern in which shopping centers, housing tracts and office parks devour farms and orchards. Current estimates say that a million acres of U.S. farmland disappears this way each year.

This disappearance, of course, worried County Executive John V.N. Klein, elected in 1972. What worried him equally was the county budget. Such rapid population growth, Klein argued, destroys the rural quality of life the refugees from urban centers are seeking. They are forced into an ersatz urban way of living, and their numbers and the suddenness with which they appear destroy any quality even that might have. Urbanization drains groundwater supplies faster than they can be replenished, for instance. And there is no way local governments can supply the services these advancing hordes demand. Faced with supplying the fire and police protection, the roads, the schools and other services needed by these burgeoning ranks of newcomers, the county could only go further into debt. There was no way Suffolk County could pay for the increases needed if the growth continued.

Klein and his staff worked out figures showing that the higher the density of development, the larger the county deficit. Even under the development densities allowed by the strictest zoning (one acre minimum lots) residential tax income would fall short of the costs of community services. So Suffolk County came up with a plan based roughly on a scheme used in Great Britain during the housing boom fol-

lowing World War II to enable farmers to keep farming their land. The Suffolk plan, which took six years of debate, study and negotiation among Suffolk residents, legislators and officials, simply allows the county to buy from farmers the development rights to their acreage. If he participates, a farmer retains ownership of his land, the right to pass it on to heirs, and the right to farm it as long as he wants. The county owns only the development rights; the farmer cannot develop his land without county approval. To raise money for these purchases, the county sold 30-year serial bonds. An initial issue of $21 million is expected to preserve upwards of 3,900 acres of farmland. Once this initial issue is exhausted, the county will ask permission for a second one, ultimately spending an estimated $55 million on the program and buying rights to as many as 15,000 acres, about half the county's remaining farmland. If a farmer elects to participate in the program, the county will pay him a price for the development rights to his land based on the difference between his land's value as farmland and what it would be worth (according to a current appraisal) as developable land.

Two things accrue to the farmer from this process. One, he has cash for his land, and it could be expected that, on his death, his family will not have to sell the land to pay inheritance taxes. Two, the value of his land is reduced, carrying, after the county purchases development rights, only its value as farmland, thus lowering the farmer's property tax. Several things accrue to the county — assuming they can pay off the interest and principal on the bond issues. They hang onto what is left of their rural atmosphere, they preserve the recreational character of the county, making a more pleasant place to live, with fresh air, fields, trees and unpolluted water, and they preserve the county's main industry: farming.

Suffolk's is a pioneering effort being watched carefully by other municipalities throughout the country and, indeed, by the federal government.

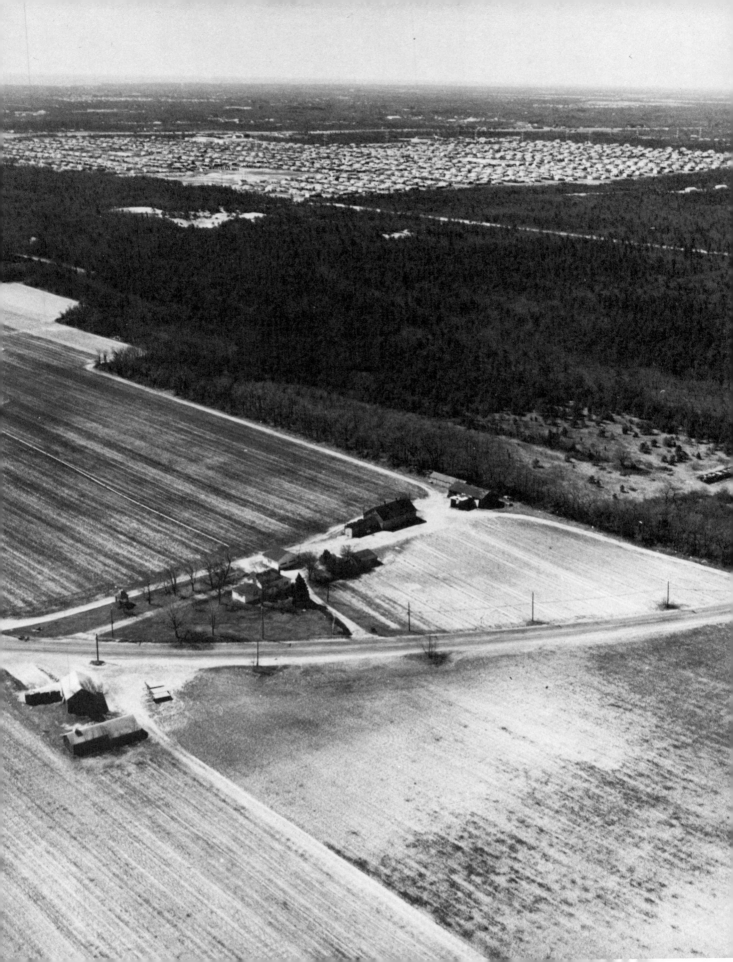

Minneapolis Neighborhood Boulevard Reforestation Plan
Minneapolis, Minn.

Designers: Minneapolis Planning Department: Oliver E. Byrum, director; Urban Design Section, Peggy Sand, principal author/designer. In cooperation with Minneapolis Park and Recreation Board and Committee on Urban Environment

Client: City of Minneapolis

For more than 50 years the streets of Minneapolis have been shaded by elms. Until a few years ago some 200,000 of these gracious trees grew in the boulevards, the grass-filled spaces between streets and sidewalks of Minneapolis neighborhoods. But as Dutch elm disease spread through the midwest, Minneapolis began losing its trees. By 1974, the city had lost 40,000 elms from along its boulevards and set out doing something about it.

That year, the Park Board's forester drew up a list of 20 varieties of trees most appropriate for boulevard replanting. Well aware of what disease could do to a single species, the city was determined to plant a diversity of trees. Indeed, the final reforestation plan, the implementation of which began in the fall of 1977, specifies that the trees in any one neighborhood shall not exceed 20 percent of any one variety nor 35 percent of any one genus.

The Minneapolis Planning Department takes some of the credit for this final diversification, though they were joined in their replacing efforts by the Minneapolis Park and Recreation Board. Together, these agencies investigated problems that would confront new trees on the block, such as phone and power lines, salt used in winter on ice and the appearance a tree would make in a particular spot. But they threw more than their own judgment into the planning pot. In most neighborhoods they went to the people living there, asking what they wanted, then spicing final plans, where possible, with individual preferences.

The program, funded by city taxes, is currently replanting 10,000 trees a year. But by 1977 the Dutch elm disease had increased until the city was losing 20,000 elms each summer along boulevards alone. Given this increase in planting sites, the reforestation may not proceed by filling each vacancy but rather by allocating a certain number of trees per community, so that new trees are distributed equally throughout the city. By preparing a plan at this point, the city can insure that reasonable supplies of the necessary young trees are available in local nurseries during the next ten to 20 years, and can advise individuals who want to plant their own boulevard trees what type to acquire. The city will try to plant the same species of tree along each residential street of from four to eight blocks.

This planting can now be done according to a master plan. The Park Board has detailed maps showing what type of tree (Hackberry, red maple, sugar maple, Norway maple, American linden, little leaf linden, pine oak, burr oak, red oak, swamp white oak, green ash, ginkgo, etc.) goes along every boulevard in the city. Once the master plan is fulfilled, the city will turn its attention to non-residential neighborhoods and parks.

A landscaping plan for downtown was released as part of the Minneapolis Metro Center report early in 1979.

Jury

Urban Design

O. Jack Mitchell
is dean of the School of Architecture at Rice University, and a consultant on land development planning and urban design projects. He previously held positions in the architecture departments at Rice and Texas A & M University, and was president of OMNIPLAN in Houston from 1970 to 1973. As partner in charge of design with Wittenberg, Delony and Davidson in Little Rock, Ark., his projects included the University of Arkansas Library in Fayetteville and the Arkansas Louisiana Gas Co. Office Building in Little Rock. Mitchell was also formerly with the offices of Caudill Rowlett Scott in Houston and Hellmuth, Obata and Kassabaum in St. Louis.

Donald L. Stull
is president of Stull Associates, Inc. He is currently on the faculty of Harvard Graduate School of Design. He has chaired the Massachusetts Building Code Commission and is currently a member of both the Design Advisory Panel and the Transit Architectural Review Board of the City of Baltimore. He serves as principal-in-charge for RAP IIA Housing, Cambridge Street Parcel 4A, Ruggles Street Station, Massport/Commonwealth Flats, all in Boston, and Salem/Derby Wharf in Salem, Mass.

Ronald Thomas
is co-director of Attic & Cellar Studios, Inc. His diverse experience includes architecture, urban design communication planning, citizen participation program development, graphic and audio/visual media design. His environmental design and planning work includes a Memphis Downtown renewal program; Jacksonville Neighborhood Development Plan; Cohoes, N.Y. Historic Preservation/Downtown Revitalization; and Chestertown, Md. Waterfront Concept. Thomas was director of an Iowa City Citizen Participation Program; a Concept for Cleveland Downtown Communications program, for which he won a Second Urban Design Awards Program selection; Pennsylvania Avenue Development Plan Public Information Media Presentation, and Operation Breakthrough User and Evaluation Photographic Study.

Alexander Cooper
is director of the Urban Design Program and adjunct professor of architecture at Columbia University. He served for five years as a member of the New York City Planning Commission, involved with citywide zoning, capital budget and community development allocations, development policy and approvals. As an urban design consultant his clients include the Rockefeller Realty Corp.; Davis, Brody and Assoc. for Kendall Square; Cambridge, Massachusetts' master plan, and the Rockefeller Family Fund. Cooper is also formerly director of the West Side Highway Office, New York City, the New York City Planning Department's Urban Design Group and director of design of the Housing and Development Administration, as well as having planned and administered many projects in cities across the nation.

Renovation and Preservation

Kenneth S. Halpern
is director of the Mayor's
Office of Midtown Planning
and Development in New
York City. He worked for
over four years in the
Mayor's Development
Office in New York and
served as project director
for a comprehensive urban
design plan for Times
Square. As a registered
architect, he has worked for
several prominent
architectural offices, was a
consultant to the Institute
for Environmental Action in
New York, has taught in
Boston, Minnesota and
New York, and was
Fulbright Professor of
Urban Design at the
Universidad de Los Andes
in Bogota, Columbia. His
book, *Downtown USA*, was
recently published by the
Whitney Library of Design.

J. Timothy Anderson
in 1961 established the firm
of Anderson Notter
Finegold, Inc., whose work
has included planning for
urban areas, designing
new structures compatible
with existing buildings and
historic environments, and
recycling old buildings for
new uses. He has served
as president of the Boston
Society of Architects and is
current president of the
Massachusetts State
Association of Architects
and an adjunct professor at
Boston University. His firm
is currently developing
plans for new living and
cultural facilities
redeveloped in the former
Charlestown Naval
Shipyard.

Anthony J. Newman
is vice president of New
York City's South Street
Seaport Museum. Among
the museum's activities are
the restoration and re-use
of the 18th and 19th
century buildings in the
South Street Seaport
Historic District. Newman
was the founding director of
the New York Landmarks
Conservancy, an
organization dedicated to
the preservation and
revitalization of
architecturally and
historically noteworthy
buildings.

Giorgio Cavaglieri
is an architect in New York
City, where he has
practiced since 1946. He
began his practice in Italy in
1936, where his projects
including a 5,000-seat
auditorium in Rome. From
1956 to 1969 he was
adjunct professor of the
School of Architecture,
Pratt Institute, in Brooklyn,
N.Y. and lecturer in city
planning at the Institute of
Design and Construction in
Brooklyn from 1949 to
1957. A former president of
the Fine Arts Federation of
New York, and of the
Municipal Art Society and
New York Chapter of the
AIA, Cavaglieri is currently
New York State
Preservation Coordinator
for the AIA. His restoration
of the Chapel of the Good
Shepherd on Roosevelt
Island, N.Y. was selected in
the Second Urban Design
Awards Program.

Index

Architects/Designers